PLAN SMART

PLAN SMART:
Conquering 10 Common Money Traps

Todd Calamita, CFP® | Chris Grobelny, MCR

ISBN-10: 0-692-73798-7

ISBN-13: 978-0-692-73798-9

Cover Design | Peter McRae

Publishing and Interior Design Services | MelindaMartin.me

PLAN SMART

CONQUERING 10 COMMON MONEY TRAPS

FINANCIAL LESSONS FROM TWO LIFE-LONG
FRIENDS, ENTREPRENEURS AND DADS

TODD CALAMITA, CFP®   CHRIS GROBELNY, MCR

Contents

Introduction

Managing your personal finances is a game you can either win or lose. Winning means you avoid debt and safeguard your future. Losing, on the other hand, ensures a lifetime of perennial money panic. The stakes could hardly be any higher.

PLAN SMART aims to fill in the gaps of what you may already know about good and bad debt, saving, investing, real estate, and planning for both a career and family. The subjects covered here are far from exhaustive but each chapter is a crucial piece of the puzzle in planning for a financially savvy life.

Why are we passionate about this? We grew up a few houses apart, started a landscaping business together at the age of ten, and in the decades since have invested in myriad investment properties together. We have learned about money as a team, through much trial and error. Our friendship is based on mutual trust and a shared love of making our money work for our families. It is our hope that the lessons we've learned in our lives will inspire our own children to make wise financial decisions.

These experiences have been the inspiration for *PLAN SMART*—to encourage our children and other young people to create good financial habits *early*. Because, let's face it: being broke sucks. It sucks when you're in your 20s and 30s, but it becomes true hardship when you are in your 40s and beyond. If you make good choices sooner rather than later—avoiding the debt trap, putting money aside for retirement, and making smart investment choices—you can achieve a life of balance and harmony.

Making your money work for you means becoming a conscious participant in your future. The fact is, being smart about money isn't brain surgery. (Don't spend what you don't make! Do you really need a BMW at 23?) But too often our culture encourages instant gratification, a buy-now-pay-later philosophy that has come to seem normal in its very pervasiveness. The decisions you make today really do matter, and our hope is that this book will encourage you to make the smart choices necessary to win the game.

About the Authors

Best friends since they were four years old, Todd Calamita and Chris Grobelny grew up ten houses apart in a tree-lined, suburban Ohio neighborhood. Summers were spent riding bikes together up and down the street, having adventures, and sharing thoughts and ideas. When they were ten, one of these ideas was to start a business.

Todd and Chris, age 14, co-owners of T & C's Landscaping

Hanging out on the front lawn of his house, Todd said, "How about we go up to Mrs. Newman's house and ask her if we can cut her grass? We could make some money." Chris was game, so they took a short walk up the street and knocked on her door. Hearing their proposal, Mrs. Newman asked what it would cost. Todd and Chris looked at each other, and Todd said, "Five bucks." Mrs. Newman agreed. They ran back to their respective houses and fired up their parents' lawnmowers. This was the moment T&C Landscaping was born.

Life was simple back then, but the concepts of choosing and working with a business partner, running a business, managing money, and dealing with people are the same at every stage of life. This was the beginning of a long-lasting relationship and the first of numerous other shared business ventures over the years.

Todd and Chris share similar values and a deep and abiding trust. The boys of T&C Landscaping are now men managing careers and family life, but they still help one another to grow and learn. The lessons within these pages contain some of that hard-won wisdom, the fruits of years spent navigating the tricky waters of business, investing, and personal finance. Now with young children of their own, the hope is that this knowledge will be a resource for the next generation.

Part I:
Starting Out Smart

In this section we will discuss how you can launch a life of financial wisdom. What will it take for you to achieve your short and long-term goals? What common missteps should you avoid? The smart money habits you create today can mean the difference between a life well-lived and one of near constant anxiety. If it seems like we are overstating this, read on for evidence to the contrary. Now that you are taking the reins of adulthood, it's time to get smart about money...and watch your dreams come to life!

Chapter 1:
Plan a Little, Save a Lot

*"If you don't know where you are
going, any road will get you there."*

—Lewis Carroll

Imagine you are having a conversation with your future self: will it be tinged with regret at not having planned and saved for the future? Or, will you look back in self-gratitude for a job well done? Because the fact is, the financial habits we create in our youth directly—and dramatically—affect our quality of life later on. It's a life skill. This is why it is crucial that you commit to a plan for financial health in the early years of your career. It doesn't have to be complex or even particularly aggressive. It just needs to commence sooner rather than later.

What are your dreams? What will it take to fulfill those dreams? What is your timeline for these goals? These questions may sound huge—and the answers will certainly change as you mature—but not asking them now means you will be floating along the currents of life rather than steering your own ship. Having no financial plan brings with it several certainties: a life mired in debt with little savings, constant anxiety that you'll get laid off, and a retirement marred by money worries. If this doesn't sound like your ideal future, read on.

The Biggie: Saving for Retirement

As hard as it may be to save when you are young, it becomes truly painful as you get older and your responsibilities grow and change. So start now. A great way to think about it: pay yourself first. No matter what your income level is you should take some of your net income before paying bills or making purchases and put it into a savings/retirement account. Whether it is a Roth IRA (taxed now) or a Traditional IRA (taxed when you access it), consistently saving from an early age will be beneficial when you are older because your money will be realized exponentially.

Another relatively painless way to save is through your employer. Many companies offer a retirement savings program and typically will incentivize employees to participate by offering some form of a match for every dollar you contribute. We say this is painless because the money can be automatically deducted from your paycheck; you won't have to *decide* to save each pay period. (When you change jobs, simply roll your 401K into an IRA or into whatever savings program your new employer offers.) If you are just starting off in your career, we recommend contributing at least 10% of your salary, if not more. Keep in mind: the more you contribute, the more you will benefit tax-wise since your taxable income will be reduced.

Paying yourself first will initially take a bit of discipline, but consider it akin to other healthy habits such as exercise and eating right: it's just something that you do to get the most out of life.

Todd Explains the Magic of Compound Interest

Whether you sock away a percentage of your salary in an IRA or 401K, these products all work according to the same idea: compound interest. Compound interest means the interest that your investment earns each year is added on to your principle. The result: your balance doesn't just increase—it increases at an exponential rate. To illustrate: if you invest $100 and the interest rate is 8%, at the end of the first year you will have $108. Invest another hundred and now your principle is $208, which at 8% becomes $224.64. Throw another $100 into the pot for your third year and you have $324.64, which at 8% becomes $350.61. Over three years, you've invested $300, and you have received $50 "for free" (the interest). With this simple math, you can see why saving from a young age makes an enormous difference down the road: the longer you play the game, the more your "free" money grows.

Let's look at the magic of compound interest over your lifetime. Congratulations! You've just gotten your first job out of college. Your starting salary of $50,000 certainly doesn't put you in the big leagues, but it's the most you've ever made, and it sure feels good. You wisely decide to put aside 12% of your salary into an IRA you won't be able to touch for decades. You commit to it even though that money would be easy to spend on any number of things—a better car, vacations, an engagement ring for your girlfriend. But you hold onto your promise to yourself and keep saving. Why? Because the payoff will be huge: if you save 12% starting at age 22 (assuming your salary increases 3% annually to account for inflation and pay raises) you will have saved around $3 million dollars by age 65. (See Appendix A for exactly how this works.) That's an investment of approximately $535,000 that magically turns into $3 million![1] Well, perhaps magic isn't really at work here, but it can certainly seem so as your balance grows and grows.

When I was 16 years old my dad took me to meet a financial advisor for the first time—and I discovered that investing was magic. I had saved up what I considered a "bunch" of money from my landscaping business. I recall sitting across from the advisor when he told me that for every $666 I invested, I would get $1000 back in four years. (Keep in mind this was the '80s and interest rates were around 12%.) I couldn't believe what I was hearing. I said, "You mean I don't have to cut lawns or do any work? They just give me back another $334?"

---

[1]   Past performance does not predict future returns.

"Yes, that's how it works."

"I'll take four of those!" I said. And that was my first official foray into investing. I ultimately kept that money locked away until I graduated college. And I'll never forget that moment of realization that my money could make money—with virtually no effort on my part! And it can for you too.

Resisting the Debt Trap

We will discuss debt—both good and bad—in detail in Chapter 3, but it is something to keep in mind as you are creating your financial plan. Some debt will be inevitable: you may have student loans to pay off or plan to take out a mortgage loan on a house or condo. Taking on a certain amount of debt can often be an effective path to achieving your dreams. But, as too many Americans know, debt obtained through high interest credit cards or car loans can be a trap from which it is difficult to escape.

Now is the time to commit to dodging the debt trap. Resist the house or car you can't really afford; take simpler vacations. Set the stage for a life free from smothering interest payments. (Remember the 'magic' we discussed above? This is the exact opposite scenario where, rather than earning, you are *paying interest on an exponentially growing balance.) If you avoid debt now, you will be less likely to get into the habit of overspending as your responsibilities grow.* This is key because the older you get, the harder it is to dig yourself out of debt or take a step down to a more affordable house or car.

Making the Plan Real

So how do you begin? With a piece of paper. You can have the best intentions of saving and avoiding debt, but if you don't write it down these promises are likely to be pushed aside by more immediate needs and desires. So grab a notebook or open a file on your computer and start dreaming. First, consider your long term goals: *If I want to retire by age 55, how much do I need to earn and how much should I set aside from those earnings? It can be useful to run different scenarios accounting for various time periods, percentages, and interest rates.* What other long-term goals do you have? Travel? Saving for your children's education? Consider these, too, as you run your numbers. If, for instance, you want to pay for your children's college, it may be more realistic to retire at 60 rather than 55.

"Wait!" you say. "I am 22 years old and have no idea if, or when, I'll have kids or how much I'll be earning in 10 or 20 years. All this planning seems crazy!" Sure, there are many unknowns. Which is why your Plan is a living document, something you can fine-tune as your life evolves. We say the only thing crazier than making a long-term plan for your financial future is *not making a long-term plan for your financial future.* Work with what you know now and go from there, keeping accountability and commitment close at hand.

Equally as empowering is planning for your short-term goals. On a separate document, write your goals for the next year, five years from now, and ten years from now. This should be fun—like making a Christmas wishlist that you give yourself. What will it be? A car? A new business venture? A trip? A graduate degree? A house? Zero balance on your Visa card? What will it take to achieve these dreams? Extra savings? Smart loans? A second job? A roommate?

Now that you've written down what you want and how you plan to get there, we suggest one more step in cementing accountability for your Plan: share it with someone. Whether it's a formal financial advisor, your mom or dad, your boyfriend or girlfriend, or simply a friend, this person can hold you indirectly accountable for achieving your goals. Just like a commitment to exercise or any other challenge, going it alone carries the risk of making silent excuses and giving up. Knowing someone is out there to hold you accountable will help you resist the temptation to prioritize everyday desires at the expense of your long-term goals.

This ability to suppress instant gratification is a true hallmark of adulthood. You are no longer the child crying for a toy or the teenager spending your pay or allowance until there's nothing left. You're on a different path now—one of financial wisdom and responsibility. Welcome!

Chris Gets a Wake Up Call

After graduating college, I took a job with a national bank in my hometown. I couldn't think of a better way to transition into the real world, living for free with my parents, working for a public company, and having very few expenses. My only liabilities were my student loans (which didn't require repayment until six months after graduation), gas for my car, and my social expenses. *Boy, I thought to myself, this is great. I am earning a paycheck and I still have a bunch of money left over!*

About a month into my new job, I was sitting at the kitchen table reading the paper when my dad came in to have his regular cup of coffee. After sitting for a moment, he looked at me and said, "Chris, we need to have a talk." *Uh oh. He walked over to his office area, came back into the kitchen, and put a stack of papers and envelopes on the table in front of me.* Dad very simply made one statement: "Pick one." I looked down at all these papers and noticed they were all bills that were due for the month. Not sure if he was kidding or not, I turned back to the newspaper and said, "Yeah, right." This was a big mistake. I then noticed the serious look my dad always gave when he meant business. This was no joke. My dad wanted me to pick one bill and be responsible for that bill every month. I don't think he really cared which bill it was, but I certainly had to pick one. Obviously, I was not picking the mortgage payment which was the largest of them all, so I looked through them and ultimately decided to pick the gas bill, as this incurs the lowest usage in summer months in Cleveland, Ohio. I figured if I could get through summer, I would not have to spend that much and I could figure out what to do in the fall.

At the time, I did not appreciate my dad's action as being as meaningful as I do now. He knew that no matter what I was making at the bank, it was more than enough to cover my student loans and basic living expenses, and he didn't want me to get too comfortable living in a house that my parents had been enjoying all to themselves the prior four years. His tactic kept me on my toes, and was a clear lesson in responsibility and what it means to have a home and pay the monthly bills. As well, it forced me to figure out my long-term plan. I did not want to be living at my folks' house when I received a raise or promotion and have Dad come to me and say: "Pick another one." I needed to take the next step in life and move out to be on my own.

I had always intended to move on with my life and buy a property of my own. In college I had made my mind up that I never wanted to rent again, as I resented writing the check to my landlord during those years with nothing to show for it at the end of the day. Soon after my dad presented me with the bills, I began searching through the local paper for a place to buy. I knew that a two-family home would be the most beneficial way for me to build equity in a property and pay a lot less toward the monthly bills if I was able to share in those expenses with a tenant.

I started driving by neighborhoods whenever I had free time and looked at properties all over town. As I narrowed down selections, I calculated the income and expense figures in my head. I wanted to make sure the rental income covered most, if not all, of my entire mortgage so that the remaining bills would be my taxes, insurance, and utilities. After about two months of looking, I made an offer on a nice Tudor-style, two-family home that I was able to finance via FHA. (FHA had certain requirements that allowed you to finance most of the purchase and come up with little down payment, as opposed to a traditional mortgage requiring a minimum of 20% down payment up front.) My thought was to have the equity build, the value of the home appreciate, and in a few years refinance with a conventional loan. This plan could not have worked out any better. I sold it for a profit six years later, and the equity built up was used to purchase my current home.

My dad put the fire under my butt to get me moving. He knew I probably would have dragged out my free ride for as long as I could. In the end, no other investment other than this piece of real estate could have provided such returns on the equity contributed. The lessons here: 1) now is the time to take responsibility for your life and do whatever it takes to move forward; 2) the earlier you can get started owning real estate and not renting, the faster it will grow for you.

Your Financial Legacy: What to Keep and What to Leave Behind

Now that you are settling into an independent life, it can be smart to take an unbiased look at your assumptions about money. The financial habits of parents have the powerful ability to carry on to the next generation. (See Chapter 5 for a deeper look at parenting and money.) Perhaps some of these you can choose to emulate: maybe your parents were smart savers who are now enjoying a stress-free retirement. Conversely, it could be your parents weren't particularly financially savvy and taught you some unfortunate lessons along the way.

As children—even as young as age five—we are constantly watching our elders. Did Mommy make spur-of-the-moment purchases to cheer herself up? Did Daddy come home with a new car every few years, then complain about the bills piling up? Were they fearful of investing, preferring to keep their savings "under the mattress" rather than reaping the rewards of a smartly diversified portfolio? Did they buy you whatever you wanted, thrilled to give you a life of abundance?

These are lessons we absorb unconsciously: *I deserve to get whatever I want. Or, I guess it's normal to buy what I want now and deal with money stress later. Or, the stock market is too risky for me. Once grown and on our own, the poor habits we've inherited from our families of origin can be difficult to shake.* Think back on your own experiences as a child: what good financial practices did you witness that you'd like to keep? What are some negative ones you can let go of? Be vigilant about this, especially during moments of big change or stress. Remember: the rewards of living a life of smart money habits go beyond just you—one day your children, too, will be watching and learning.

• •

Embracing adult responsibility should feel empowering; taking charge of your money and your life is a real source of pride. As you read on, keep your Plan close at hand as the following chapters may spark some ideas.

Pearls of Wisdom

- Start saving for retirement now.
- Avoiding "bad" debt at a young age can save you from the debt trap later.
- Write down and give voice to your financial Plan.
- Steer your money habits away from negative family legacies.
- Embrace responsibility!

Chapter 2:
Living Within Your
Means in a World of
Wants vs. Needs

"A budget is telling your money
where to go instead of
wondering where it went."

– Dave Ramsey

Every once in a while, in a magazine or on the Internet, there's a feature on an "amazing" person: **Young couple pays off mortgage in eight years!** Man makes $200k, chooses to live on $50k! Fortune 500 executive drives used Honda! There's a reason why headlines like these make national news in the United States. Voluntarily spending a lot less than we make or aggressively saving money is just not what our culture encourages. And unfortunately, stories like these do seem to represent an extreme choice—many people are spending more than they make, not less. And they are definitely not aggressively tackling debts. We call this *not* living within your means.

As you go over your budget, get real with your needs versus wants. Maslow's Hierarchy of Needs (pictured below) is a great place to start. If you take Maslow's philosophy to heart, you won't feel denied or deprived when realizing which things in your life are unnecessary wants; it should feel liberating. We define living within your means as spending your money with conscious deliberation (rather than on impulse). If you have the surplus cash to afford a fancy vacation, and travel is important to you, go for it. But if that trip (a *want*) is going to sink you into debt or make it difficult for you to meet your *needs*, it is smarter to skip it or opt for a more modest travel option.

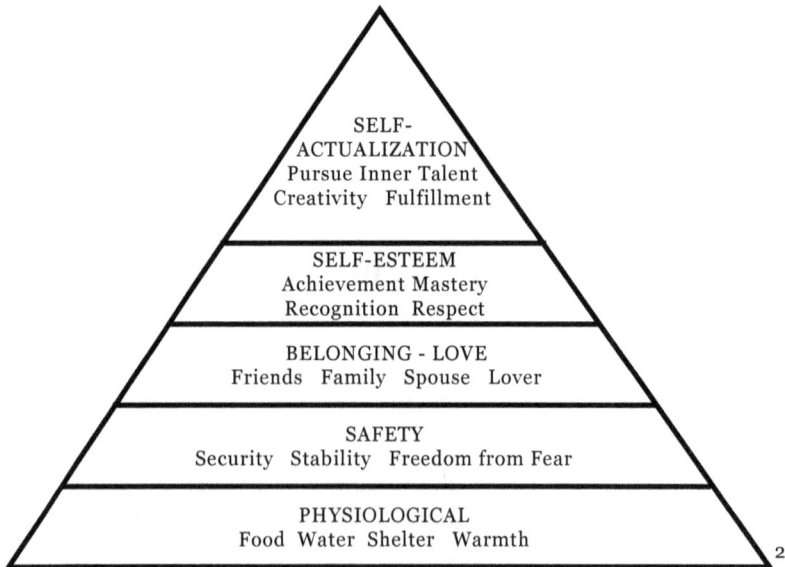

```
                    SELF-
                 ACTUALIZATION
                Pursue Inner Talent
              Creativity  Fulfillment

                 SELF-ESTEEM
              Achievement Mastery
              Recognition  Respect

               BELONGING - LOVE
            Friends  Family  Spouse  Lover

                    SAFETY
          Security  Stability  Freedom from Fear

                 PHYSIOLOGICAL
            Food  Water  Shelter  Warmth               2
```

2 http://www.simplypsychology.org/maslow.html

What "Living Within Your Means" Looks Like in Chris's Life

A lot of people get in over their heads with investments or purchases that can get them into trouble when less rosy times strike. For me, living within my means involves believing tougher times could be around any corner—and that's because they are! I don't see this as being paranoid, simply realistic. Besides the everyday "whammies" of car troubles, leaky roofs, and other unexpected—if minor—calamities, there are bigger patterns of risk at work. According to the International Monetary Fund, there has been a pattern of recession in advanced economies in recent decades, the most recent one being one of the worst since the Great Depression.[3] History proves that the good times are always balanced out eventually.

This attitude of "expect the best, but also anticipate the worst" can be applied to almost every financial choice you make, and it is a key tool in helping stay financially healthy by having a preparation mindset. It's great to afford the big, beautiful house today—but what if you and your wife have a baby and one of you wants to stay home? Will you be able to dig yourself out of the debt burden?

I know achieving total freedom from debt is the goal of many people. It's a great goal for sure. However, my own approach is a bit softer, as I like my life to feel more balanced. I'd rather spread out debt over the

---

3   Claessens, Stijn and M. Ayhan Kose. "Recession: When Bad Times Prevail," IMF 3/28/2012.

course of my life and feel reasonably comfortable all the time rather than hunker down and live sparingly for years now, eventually feeling free years later. Debt is not a problem, if managed appropriately. I have debt and would like it to disappear, but it doesn't scare me. That's my comfort level, and only you can decide how you want to live. The important part, though, is the *deciding*. I've made a conscious choice about how to manage money and debt in my life, and I'm always revisiting it, checking my spreadsheets and Quicken to make sure things are on track. You can't go on cruise control or put your head in the sand; the choices, no matter what they are, must be conscious ones.

What "Living Within Your Means" Looks Like in Todd's Life

My basic definition of living within your means is to spend less than you make. For most people, that is difficult. When I go through a client's budget and expenses, I always try to structure his or her financial plan so the client is not only not spending more than what's coming in, but also a minimum of 10 percent of their income is going toward retirement. Put together a written retirement plan (ideally with the help of someone who can hold you accountable), so that you know what the impact will be on your life when you are ready to retire.

The house and the car are where most people are living beyond their means. I see too many people paying as much as 50 percent of their take-home pay on their house and as much as 25 percent of their take-home pay on a car payment. Are debt and credit overuse and abuse just the American way these days? Perhaps. Americans are used to instant gratification. Now, kids are growing up seeing that their parents can borrow money to get what they want, when they want it. It's a vicious cycle. Even after the housing crash of 2008, getting access to credit of all kinds is still relatively easy in the United States. Credit card companies are on campuses signing up college students who don't even have an income yet!

And what about car purchases? For many people, walking into a car dealership with the expectation of taking on a loan for a new car is the norm. A monthly car payment is simply another bill to pay. It is the utter normalcy of this that blinds today's consumers to the pitfalls of taking on a car loan. Besides the obvious perils of interest payments, it is tempting to purchase a more expensive car than you actually need when you don't pay cash. This is understandable. On the lot, with the salesman working his charms, it is easy to justify buying a sleek new foreign car with all the bells and whistles. What's an extra $25, $50, or $100 per month? The fact is, if you were actually forced to save $30,000 for a car, you would likely buy a less expensive model. And, over the course of a lifetime, the money you spend on new cars (that depreciate by 10% almost instantly, and lose 15-20% of their value each year after purchase[4]), plus interest costs, adds up significantly.

4   http://auto.howstuffworks.com/under-the-hood/cost-of-car-ownership/car-depreciation1.htm

The investment management team at Muhlenkamp did an interesting exercise: assuming that over the course of a lifetime you save $2,000 per year by paying cash for *used* vehicles, you can become a millionaire in 36 years. The logic: if you invested that money in an IRA (compounded at 12%), it would eventually grow to over $1 million.

While this simple math may make that used Honda Accord a bit more attractive, saving your money to buy a car will still feel like swimming against the societal tide. Let's face it: it's easier to borrow what you don't have than to save up. These loans are easy to get, and everyone is doing it. And the real kicker: you don't want to be embarrassed by your ride. There's real pressure in our consumer-driven society to drive a nice car. What will your boss think? Your date? Her dad? These feelings are difficult to conquer. But think about the peace of mind you would feel driving a less expensive car and knowing that you are on a path to wealth. By choosing not to be part of the culture of buy-now-pay-later, you *will* be in the minority, and for some people, that can feel uncomfortable. It's hard, but don't let direct or indirect peer pressure do that to you. Believe me: the Joneses are more than likely living in a sea of debt.

Another thing about the Joneses: just as you can choose not to keep up with them, you can also choose not to live with them. If you hang out with people who veer toward being materialistic or are comfortable with big spending, consider making new friends or moving to a less expensive neighborhood. That may sound drastic, but it is similar to going on a diet: it's a lot harder to do when you are around people who don't eat right or exercise.

Todd Explains Why Accountability Matters

I have found accountability to be another key to achieving financial harmony. You can tell yourself stories all day long about how you need that expensive car or dinner out, but having an advisor—formal or informal—can help you choose to spend more responsibly.

Some years ago, I participated in a local news station's financial boot camp. The show matched financial advisors with people seeking to get their finances in order. I was paired with Donna, a single mom making $50,000 per year who was trying to pay her daughter's way through school. At our first meeting, she shared with me that her goal was to "get a better grip on how to manage money."

I recall that Donna was open to doing whatever I suggested because she was so determined to correct the situation, but she didn't know where to start. She was overwhelmed. My homework for her was to write down all of her expenses in detail, not to use a credit card, and pay for everything in cash. We worked together for about three months, meeting every few weeks to review her expenses and talk about ways to reduce or eliminate certain expenses. I remember her saying how much she liked sushi, but she also realized how expensive it was to eat out. After the three months, it seemed to me that

Donna's biggest challenge to continue spending within her means was accountability. She had great respect for her brother and he managed his money wisely. So we brought him into the conversation and he agreed to meet with her monthly and hold her accountable. Like a diet or an exercise program, it sometimes takes accountability to stay focused on your goals.

Budgeting with Buckets

Whether trying to save money or lose weight, there is no one-size-fits-all solution. However, as with dieting, sometimes the financial strategies that work best are a little offbeat, even fun. One of these effective savings strategies is the "bucket concept." Rather than adhere to the traditional budgeting chore of writing down expenses and tracking them each month, the bucket concept suggests dividing spending into six categories and assigning a specific percentage to each bucket as follows:

- Allocate 50 percent for necessities, including groceries, mortgage payments, car payments, utilities, gas, Internet, cell phone bills, and anything else you "need."

- Mark 10 percent for long-term savings to fund vacations, car repairs, house maintenance, clothing, and other items you may not necessarily need to spend money on each month.

- Put 10 percent into retirement accounts such as a 401(k) plan or IRAs.

- Spend 10 percent on activities or items you enjoy. Whether it's dining out, a trip to the theater, or an afternoon of golf with friends, allow yourself to have a bucket in your budget for things that make you happy and enrich your life.

- Reserve 10 percent for education needs, such as paying off student loans, saving for your children's college education, or continuing personal development.

- Donate 10 percent to charity.

When making allocations to each bucket, consider 100 percent of your total after-tax income. This means that in addition to income earned, you also divide inheritances, bonuses, and even your tax refund into six categories. The key is that this money should never be commingled. The easiest way to fund each bucket is to open separate checking accounts and have the appropriate percentage of your paycheck deposited into each account.

In discussing the bucket concept with clients, there are some common reactions. Most notably, many say they spend far more than 50 percent of their income on necessities. Naturally, you can adjust the percentages to reflect your own circumstances. For example, if you need 65 percent for necessities, you might drop education, charity, and long-term savings to 5 percent.

However, I encourage you to at least reflect on the possibility of living on 50 percent of your income. Often, simply considering this idea can help people begin to prioritize expenses and think more proactively about how they're spending money each month. In fact, quite a few clients have realized they were living in homes that were too expensive for them.

Debt is another issue that can throw a wrench into your ideal percentages. If you have significant consumer debt, you may need to direct more than 50 percent to the necessities bucket in order to help dig out of the debt hole as soon as possible. However, once you're out of debt, funding a long-term savings account can help you stay debt free. That is, as your long-term savings builds over time, you'll have a cushion so you won't have to use plastic to manage an unexpected car or home-repair bill. In that sense, long-term savings also can function as the traditional "emergency account."

You may be surprised to learn that the most important part of this plan is to spend the fun money on a regular basis and not accumulate it for more than 90 days. The premise being that most budget plans fail because they create a spending plan that is too tight for comfort. Think of spending money on yourself as both a reward for saving and as a means of re-energizing your motivation to save more. Regardless of whether you choose to develop a "bucket" budgeting strategy, remember that using a budget is one of the best ways to maintain your financial health.

Do Away With Your Lump Sum Payments

Many people choose to pay bills like car insurance, homeowner insurance, life insurance, disability insurance, property taxes, gym memberships, subscription services, and other one-time, annual expenses as a lump sum payment when the bill is due. On the surface, that makes financial sense. The reality is that most people don't put enough money away on a monthly basis for it to be available by the time the bill is due. The result: an unrealistic view of how much money they actually have to spend each month. Instead of putting away an extra $200-500/month for these types of expenses, this money ends up being spent on things they may want but don't need, and when the bill finally arrives, it needs to be paid with a credit card or a line of credit. In other words, money they don't actually have.

Despite it costing slightly less to pay these bills one time a year, in the long run it typically costs more. By breaking out your annual expenses on a monthly basis, it simplifies the budgeting process so you don't have to plan for these large expenses, especially since there are often other large, one-time expenses that come up throughout the year that you can't plan for, like home and car repairs.

● ●

We all know deep down that money doesn't buy happiness, but goodness, don't so many of us try anyway! The fact is, according to a recent study by two Princeton University researchers, the happiness threshold seems to be an income of $75,000. Making more money than that will not necessarily increase your happiness. The gist of the study: this relatively modest income allows most people to afford the basics and focus on their relationships and health. Buying more gizmos or the fabulous vacations you can afford with a higher payday doesn't actually increase day-to-day happiness.[5] Even if you've got millions, we encourage everyone to savor the things money can't buy. You should be able to have a lot of love, and a lot of fun adventures, without spending very much money.

Pearls of Wisdom

- Hope for the best, but anticipate the worst.
- Make a conscious choice about how much debt you are comfortable with.
- Avoid the Joneses: decide to eschew the culture of instant gratification.
- Filling your "buckets" to reflect your circumstances is a fun way to budget.
- Focus on what is actually meaningful in your life: family, relationships, simple pleasures, giving back.

5   Rubin, Courtney. "At What Price Happiness? $75,000." Inc. 9/7/10.

Chapter 3:
The Good and Bad of Debt

"A man in debt is so far a slave."

– Ralph Waldo Emerson

A funny thing about the word debt: one would think the definition is pretty black and white, but the truth is, everyone draws the line in a different place. So we'll start with how we define debt, and we urge you to adopt our definition from today forward.

Debt is money that you owe. Furthermore, if you don't pay toward that debt, you may lose the material item it represents or receive an ugly jolt to your credit rating. A car payment is definitely debt. A mortgage is a debt—yes, even if you pay it in full every month. Even an apartment lease represents a potential debt: Move out early, and you'll owe the remaining amount on the lease to finish the year. Your credit card bill with more than a $0 balance is a debt. That outstanding $30 bill from a dentist appointment four years ago that pops up on your credit report—a debt. Student loans are debts. "Liability" is a fancier word for debt, but it's all the same stuff.

We all know, reflexively, that debt is "bad," especially when it comes to credit card debt, with its jumbo interest rates and the way the industry (if not our society at large) encourages paying the minimum now as a way to "get ahead." We'll go through the troubling side of debt first. But then we'll also explore the good side of having liabilities as part of your Plan. Debt, when used in a savvy way, can be helpful. It's all about having the financial knowhow and commitment to manage that debt and stay on top of it.

Recession Woes: Chris's Experience with Debt

Ah, the American dream. My family was certainly living it: I had a good job at a commercial real estate firm and enjoyed generous regular bonuses; Todd and I were excited about several promising real estate investments; Maria and I enjoyed our nice Colonial in a good neighborhood; and my children attended private school. There were vacations, meals out—nothing extravagant, but we weren't scrimping either.

Then it hit: the Great Recession of 2008. And suddenly the ground, which before had felt so solid, seemed to give way. It was awful and amazing to see how fast the crisis went from a headline to something that directly affected my life—and the lives of so many others. It felt as if each day another colleague was downsized, and morale at work had never been worse. Bonuses were now a fond memory, but I couldn't complain. I was lucky to still have a job. And boy did we need it— Maria had just given birth to our third child and had left her job to stay at home. It was a lot for one income to manage.

During those years between 2008 and 2011 debt became a new reality for us. I watched the "sound" real estate investments Todd and I had made flounder, and it hurt. Like another person sitting at our dinner table, debt was a permanent fixture that affected everything. Meals out, vacations, and frivolous expenses were no longer a possibility. The mantra at our house became *simple living*. And, to be honest, this wasn't all a bad thing. I was reminded that, beyond the basics of health, food, and shelter, we didn't need a whole lot of big-ticket items to be happy. Though, I will admit that there was one expense Maria and I were not willing to give up—Juliana's and Nicholas' (and eventually Michael's) private school. We felt so strongly about this, we were willing to make additional sacrifices to ensure we could afford it. Everyone has their priorities, the one or two things they just can't let go of, even in the leanest of times. (Just be sure what you prioritize is in line with your values. A commitment to paying for continuing education courses is smart; a big car payment on your fancy ride is probably unnecessary.)

As the economy improved, my family's finances slowly recovered. I was committed to steadily paying off the debts we had accrued until all that was left were our personal mortgage and investment properties—

liabilities I was comfortable with. Even now, the lessons of the Great Recession linger and we tend to be more frugal remembering the pain of that time.

Avoiding Debt

The burden of debt can affect more than just your financial life. It carries a significant emotional and physical toll and can erode your confidence, delaying some of life's key milestones such as launching a business, getting married, starting a family, and buying a home. Even more troubling, a recent study analyzed over 8,000 young adults between 24 and 32 years old and found that those carrying significant debt were more likely to have poor health, including high blood pressure. "You wouldn't necessarily expect to see associations between debt and physical health in people who are so young," said Elizabeth Sweet, lead author of the study. "Our study is just a first peek at how debt may impact physical health."[6] Given these repercussions, the wisdom of avoiding debt entirely seems obvious.

Of course, sometimes debt can be a necessary burden (think school loans and mortgages), but there are ways to avoid making the easy mistakes that so often trip us up. Here are five realistic habits that we suggest everyone adopt in order to avoid becoming mired in debt.

---

6   Elizabeth Sweet, Arijit Nandi, Emma K. Adam, Thomas W. McDade. "The high price of debt: Household financial debt and its impact on mental and physical health." *Social Science & Medicine*, Volume 91, Issue null, Pages 94-100.

- Track what you spend.

- If you are in a relationship, hold each other accountable by discussing large purchases before they are made. It is wise to set a dollar amount at which the proposed purchase must be discussed. For some people this could be $100, for others much more. The key is to set the terms and stick with that agreement.

- Decide ahead of time how much you want to spend on a certain item *before* going to the store/online. Or, determine for the year how much you want to spend on large-ticket items such as vacations and home improvement.

- Don't put anything on credit.

- Do not make spontaneous large purchases. Sleep on it first and then decide if you really want to spend the money—even if you have the money to spend!

Todd Feels the Weight of Debt

Here are some scary facts: as of December 2015, American consumers owed $12.12 trillion in debt. The two largest sources of this massive number are mortgage and student loan debt, with credit card debt coming in third with $733 billion owed. If these numbers are hard to fathom, consider this breakdown: the average U.S. household owes $5,883 on their credit cards.[7] For some, rather than relying on credit cards, they are dipping into their home equity lines as another source of income. The numbers prove the story. In 2015 home-equity loan activity rose 20% over the prior year and is the third straight year at that level or higher.[8] As a society, we are living in denial. Carrying significant personal debt—to the detriment of our financial, emotional, and physical health—has come to seem almost normal, a way of life.

When I was young, debt didn't faze me, especially if it was a business debt. That view didn't come from a place of naïveté or over-confidence, but from experience: I'd had debts before, like the loan I took out to buy a truck for my landscaping business as a teen, and I'd been successful in not only paying the money back but using debt as a tool to make more money than I owed. The same was true of my early experiences buying real estate: buy a property, do some fixing up, rent it (and enjoy relatively passive income), or sell it and enjoy a profit.

Needless to say, I would soon learn that those simple principles are much more complex. As you will read about in my tale of starting the wine business in Chapter 10, I took on considerable debt and later left my bank position for self-employment. When I saw money wasn't coming in to pay off debt like it had previously for me, well, it was absolutely one of the

7   Chen, Tim. "American Household Credit Card Debt Statistics: 2014" http://www.nerdwallet.com/blog/credit-card-data/average-credit-card-debt-household/

8   Davidson, Paul. "Home equity credit lines boom 20% in 2015 in borrowing binge". http://www.usatoday.com/story/money/2016/03/28/home-equity-credit-line-boom-20-2015-borrowing-binge/82259484.

most stressful periods of my life. Here I was, someone who'd never lived beyond his means, and who took on debts with good intentions of launching businesses, but still it happened: The weight of the debt made me feel paranoid about every $10. It was out of the question to go out to eat or to take a trip somewhere by plane.

It felt never-ending, and I know well that terrible sense that there's no freedom with money: every time I bought something, I wondered, *How will I pay for this?* I knew to be successful as a financial advisor, I needed to be the sort of person who could tackle debt and not lose sight of the big picture. When I did finally pay everything off, now almost a decade ago, it was the most freeing feeling. It was like I had a new lease on life. I hope you take heart in knowing that I understand the feelings of fear and being overwhelmed, and I also know that just as patience and perspective got me through it, it can get you through it, too. Don't give up!

When You're in Too Deep

Unfortunately, finding yourself in the quicksand of debt is an all too common experience these days. At first glance, one would assume that a young person just beginning a career would be somewhat immune to debt accumulation. After all, most young 20-somethings lack the big expenses that come along later in life—kids, mortgages, medical needs. But a combination of student loan debt and aggressive credit card companies that target college students quickly proves this assumption wrong. A study that polled 20,000

Millennials concluded that young people are carrying a huge burden of non-asset building loans such as credit card debt, lines of credit, and car payments.[9] Some analysts blame a poor job market, while others fault our consumer-driven, buy-now-pay-later society. Whatever the reason, it's never too late to fight your way out of debt—no matter how bottomless it feels.

Should you find yourself in this situation, the key is to take baby steps. First, go ahead and tear up those credit cards. No more purchasing items unless you have the *actual* cash to do so. Then prioritize which debts you'd like to pay off—begin by tackling the card with the highest interest rate and work your way down from there. You may be thinking this all seems impossible, given mammoth interest rates and a limited income. If so, it's time to look at your cash flow and figure out how you can either cut your spending or make extra money. Can you get another roommate to help out with housing costs? What about trading in for a lower car payment? Or, take the bus. Perhaps get a second job while you are getting your head above water. Do some research—is it possible to get a deferment or forbearance on your student loan, at least for the time being? And avoid unnecessary expenses such as eating out and vacations.

While none of these solutions is fun, the point is that it is crucial to do everything possible to reduce your bad debt and the harmful financial, emotional, and physical repercussions it can have on your life. Besides, living a

9   "Why Gen Y is losing the debt battle." msn.com. 5/10/13. http://money.msn.com/saving-money-tips/post.aspx?post=6b52d181-15db-4ddc-8463-4e8501585d3d

debt-free life can mean massive benefits for your long-term wealth. Think about it this way: every dollar that goes toward your interest payments could instead be bolstering your retirement account. And wouldn't you rather invest in your future than simply handing your money over to MasterCard?

There is one path to becoming debt-free that we do not recommend—declaring bankruptcy. In most circumstances, becoming this deeply mired in debt is the result of a series of poor choices, poor planning, and bad luck. If you feel yourself headed down this path, do your best to turn the ship around before it's too late. Bankruptcy is a last resort option that leaves a black mark on your credit for 10 years and can also negatively affect your self-esteem. No matter how deep your debt, there is value in owning up to what you owe rather than taking the easy way out. A better option for the most severe cases of bad debt is negotiating with creditors for better terms or consulting a credit counselor. This can be a smart way to get the ball rolling.

The Good Side of Debt

We believe in debt for the right reasons—or, making your money work for you, rather than you working for your money. This can mean making sound choices—even if there is risk involved—about investing in a home, a business, or your education. Or, it can mean putting your money to profitable use rather than paying off a low-interest bearing debt.

Buying a home or investing in real estate will likely necessitate a hefty bank loan. Smart research about what and where you are buying, depending on current interest rates, can make borrowing this money a no-brainer—you're building equity while avoiding paying rent. (See Chapter 9 on real estate investing for more information on this subject.)

As well, getting a loan to start a business can be a good strategy for building your career. Just be sure to keep in mind the alternatives for paying back the debt if the business fails. Indeed, this debt could become your personal burden. If you keep this fact in the back of your mind, you may make more prudent choices when it comes to the amount of money you borrow in the first place. A thorough business plan and understanding of your field will be key to minimizing risk in this situation. Remember: it's easy to get carried away and buy things you don't necessarily need to get your company up and running. Spend as little as you can to get your business started and build it step by step. Borrowing to fund a specific business need can also be a smart way to make more money in the end—if your work demands faster computers, an upgraded kitchen, a more reliable truck, these items can eventually be paid off and will help increase overall profits.

Borrowing money for college and graduate school can also be a sound investment in your future. Of course, seek scholarships and grants if they are available to you, but student loans can make sense if you are working toward a degree that will enable you to land a job in a field that you love. Obviously, there can be a mismatch here if you take out a giant loan to seek a career that doesn't necessarily pay well. Don't go to Harvard if you want to be a kindergarten teacher—you will be capped out at a certain salary that will make paying off your student loan insurmountable.

Borrowing money can bolster your ability to excel at your career, build your home equity, and grow your investment portfolio. With a little bit of luck and plenty of hard work, hopefully the good debts you acquire (and pay off) will help you to achieve the ultimate goal: a liability-free retirement.

• •

Of course, as we know, real estate bubbles can burst and businesses fail. You could lose your job or face a medical crisis. Life is full of uncertainties. For us, the only way we know to mitigate these risks is to live life thoughtfully, ask for support when we need it, and remain conscious of every decision we make. Debt is not a good place to let your heart lead the way. This philosophy can be especially helpful as you navigate the choppy waters of good and bad debt. Good luck!

Pearls of Wisdom

- Avoiding bad debt is much simpler than getting rid of it.

- Don't panic if you are deep in debt. Take the necessary steps to get out of it.

- Don't wait to get out of debt—start now.
- Understand the difference between good and bad debt.
- Take on each debt thoughtfully, rather than letting your emotions lead the way.

Part II:
Money and Family

No matter your present relationship status, a financial life typically doesn't happen in a vacuum. You may marry in your 20s or later in life, have a small or sprawling family, buy one house or several. All of these life events mean rethinking - and successfully communicating—your financial goals. In this section, we will explore how to handle your money in the domestic sphere—another piece of the larger financial puzzle of your life. In our collective experience, change is the only constant when it comes to family, so remaining vigilant about managing your money as your circumstances shift is crucial.

Chapter 4:
Merging Your Financial
Goals with Your Spouse

"You aren't wealthy until you have
something money can't buy."

– Garth Brooks

The intersection of money and love can be a source of tension in a romantic relationship. Agreeing on how to share the financial burden of your family is tricky—after all, we each come to the table with preconceived notions about money, as well as expectations of how our futures will look. Whether you hope to get married someday, are involved in a serious relationship, or have already walked down the aisle, financial self-awareness and communication skills are crucial to maintaining a happy partnership.

Finding financial harmony within a committed relationship, like all things that count, takes some effort. Many couples, even happy ones who generally see eye-to-eye, have differences when it comes to money. Arguing itself isn't the problem; the difficulty lies in correctly identifying and then resolving the emotions you or your partner tie to money. And it's not about income level—whether you are making $40,000 a year or $400,000, fights about money are almost always about some other underlying issue. Maybe your wife was hurt you didn't buy her a birthday present and she took out her anger by racking up credit card purchases. Perhaps your husband felt wounded when you criticized him in front of a colleague and his reaction was to pick a fight about the cell phone bill. More often than not, money conflict is a stand-in for more complex feelings about power, self-worth and value, control, and trust.

Indeed, allowing your financial differences to go unchecked can lead to long-term marriage dissatisfaction—even divorce. According to the National Marriage Project, which provides research on the health of marriage in the U.S., "Couples who reported disagreeing about finances once a week were over 30 percent more likely to divorce over time than couples who reported disagreeing about finances a few times per month."[10] How you manage your money, how much debt you are comfortable with, and how you envision your financial future are all deeply ingrained. If you and your spouse have contradictory attitudes about these issues, it can be challenging to agree on what a healthy financial life looks like.

So how can you best protect your relationship from the pitfall of financial disputes? Ultimately, marriage can and should be pretty wonderful. Money talk can feel like

10 Ni, Preston. "How Money Issues Predict Divorce (& How to Prevent Them)" Psychology Today, 4/14/13.

a romance-killer, but we encourage you to view it as the opposite: Successful financial management within your relationship, including learning to understand each other's view of money, is imperative for a marriage's success. Planning a big trip together, buying a new house, figuring out how to create a financial safety net so one spouse can pursue a dream—these can be pivotal moments in a relationship, where marriage is about teamwork in a clear, tangible way. And teamwork and trust is what it's all about, isn't it?

We'll talk about several ways to manage money in a relationship in this chapter, and look at ways real marriages (including our own) have handled bends in the road.

Before You Say "I Do"

When a couple is newly enthralled with one another, they often *underestimate* how different beliefs about money can damage a marriage and *overestimate* the hope that feelings of love will carry them through differences. Many couples have simplistic conversations about money before they get married: "Are you a spender or a saver?" is a good start, but doesn't delve nearly deep enough.

First, don't assume you define the words "spender" and "saver" in the same way. That's why such questions should prompt a conversation, not just one-sentence answers. If asked, most people would describe their grocery shopping habits as "average." But the real story is in the definition: One person's regular routine is clipping coupons before hitting Walmart once a month; for another person, it's normal to load up at Whole Foods every week, grabbing pricey prepared foods from the deli. Neither choice is right or wrong. But to learn what someone considers "average," you're going to have to dig a bit.

People may also have different definitions of the terms "debt" and "affordable." If you've been saving nickels and dimes to buy a good used car outright, you may be shocked if your partner wants to borrow $15,000 for that same vehicle: "A car payment's not really a debt. It's just part of getting ahead." He may categorize debt as money owed to credit cards or unpaid bills. For him, and as misguided as it may be, a car payment is just an inevitable part of life, like a water or heating bill. These are the kinds of assumptions that you need to mine for early on in a relationship in order to avoid future quarrels—or at the very least, hash out your differences before there are other pressures (kids, mortgage) in the picture.

Many couples get married and don't realize until later that they have an entirely divergent view of money. Sometimes that's due to rose-colored glasses. Psychologists also say there are some mating rituals at play: Perhaps we pretend, a little, to be a fastidious housekeeper or a lavish spender because we know our future spouse values those habits. Once married, that front will start to slide away. Then we may end up feeling trapped in the marriage or blindsided by our mate's 'new' and unforeseen qualities.

"We love each other—it will all work out" isn't a solid financial plan. Below is a list of money-related questions to explore up front, before you tie the knot. Hopefully they will prompt an honest discussion that can drastically improve your chances of enjoying a long, nurturing marriage.

How did your parents deal with money?

What financial habits of your parents do you emulate?

- What are your earliest memories or experiences involving money?

- What is your credit score?

- Have you ever been late on a payment or had a service (phone, cable) disconnected? What was going on then?

- Do you have an emergency fund? How much is in it?

- Are you saving for retirement? If so, what percentage of your income?

- How do you imagine retirement?

- How much of a down payment would you want to put down on a car or a house?

- How much do you pay in rent/mortgage, and what percentage of your income is that?

- What do you consider a debt? Is a car payment a debt?

- How do you feel about debt?

- Did you pay for college yourself? Do you think we should pay some or all college costs for our kids? How much?

- How did your parents help you financially when you were a teenager, in college, and after college?

- Did you buy your first car or did your parents?

- Did you work in high school or college?

- How do you feel about charitable giving?

- What's the most expensive purchase you've ever made? How did you save for it or pay it off?

- Describe a friend or family member who you consider good with money. Why? Describe a friend or family member who you consider bad with money. Why? If one person is making most or all of the money, does that person get to make most or all of the financial decisions?

- How do you define work?

- What level of affluence do we want as a couple?

- If the path to a certain level of affluence requires enormous work hours (think of an investment banker or corporate attorney working 70 hours a week) and thus a lot of time apart, is that OK? What will we do if it stops being OK?

- Do we want to have kids? How many? Would one spouse stay home, and if so, for how long? How much does daycare cost a month?

- How do you think about money and gender? Do you view men as primary financial providers? Do you consider women who earn more than their spouses to be threatening? Is one spouse responsible for providing a certain lifestyle to the other?

Divorce rates being what they are, some engaged couples wonder whether signing a prenuptial agreement is prudent. We say, unless you are a multi millionaire, there is a better way. Rather than having a formal pre-nup—which can cause tension and a damaging environment of mine vs. yours so early in the partnership—create a written, non-legally binding document that outlines what you both want the financial part of your relationship to look like. Use the questions above to brainstorm and then—together— create a written blueprint to save, spend, and pursue your dreams. This document will change along with your circumstances, so keep revisiting it in order to remain on the same page going forward.

The Long and Winding Road

Gone through all these questions with no red flags? Headed out on your honeymoon? Congratulations! And now we get to the big, giant "but." While it's all well and good to make a financial plan together before marriage, surprises await. Feelings about money shift as we age. Feelings about money can *really* shift if children enter the picture. People who adored their careers at 29 sometimes want to go back to school and try something new at 37. The house in the so-so school district that seemed cool and hip before kids, can seem very wrong once your family has grown. You just don't know what awaits you. No one can foresee how his beliefs about money and work are going to change. It just happens.

So what can you do? Marriage involves faith. But it's an educated faith. You're signing up for the person, not the plan. Plans change, but if you have an excellent sense of your spouse's character and values, you stand a much better chance of weathering bends in the road together.

Todd and Teresa Change Course

When Teresa and I were first married, she relocated from Houston to Charlotte to begin our life here together. I was ecstatic when we finally packed up her house and drove the U-Haul across country to Charlotte. But those first six months were tough: Teresa worked long hours from home for an IT company and was constantly traveling to far-flung client sites. She was exhausted and unhappy as we both adjusted to the newness of being married and living under one roof. I finally suggested she quit her job and seek a fresh start. She had about $20k in backup money in her savings account, and I felt like I was going to be earning more money at my job as a financial advisor. We wouldn't have guessed we'd be making changes like this so early in the marriage, but we decided the choices were best for our team of two.

At this same time, she and I had been investing in real estate and taking advantage of the boom in Charlotte. We had flipped a few townhomes and a residential lot and were usually on the same page when it came to choosing the right properties. When Chris and I were going to renovate a house in one of the up-and-coming neighborhoods, I suggested Teresa get her real estate license and take on more of a full time role in finding properties and managing the rehabs. She got her broker's license while she was working and quit her job not long afterwards.

Teresa soon began seeking out investment properties. We had already run the numbers and basically knew how many houses we would need to flip in order to duplicate her income. On paper, it made sense: my earnings would grow as a financial advisor and we would share in this fun side business where Teresa would thrive. But there was a twist we hadn't foreseen: working together. In any relationship, it takes time and a lot of trial and error to appreciate one another's ideal communication style. For Teresa and me—two very different people very much in love—this challenge would have still been plenty interesting had we kept our jobs separate. But commingling our work lives meant that my natural directness came off as bossy and rude while her tendency towards quiet thoughtfulness struck me as indecisive. And unlike other colleagues with whom we could dispassionately disagree, the conflicts between us were fraught.

After a month or so, it became clear that we were not able to work together in real estate. When she began working for a different client who specialized in commercial properties, we still had the same disagreements. In the meantime, my business wasn't growing as quickly as I had hoped, so we were depleting Teresa's savings rapidly. As you can probably guess, it was a stressful time—and we were supposed to be carefree newlyweds, or so everyone says, right?

Ultimately it was Teresa who saw the light: in order to be happy together, we needed to work apart. Relieved to be shifting course, she soon found a job in project management at a large national bank. Meanwhile, my business grew, and we began to recover financially. Most importantly, we emerged from the experience with a better understanding of how we both operate. We both learned to blame each other less, to support each other more, and to listen with open hearts. It sounds so simple, and in some ways it is, but those three skills are still part of what keeps our family emotionally healthy day-to-day.

For many people, starting a business or working together with a spouse can be ideal—you are working towards the same goals, have your heads in the same game. Teresa and I agree that if we were to work together tomorrow, after 10 years of marriage, it would likely be a happier experience. But keep in mind: first establishing specific roles within the work environment where everyone feels comfortable is crucial. And it is much easier to do this once your roles—and best communication practices—in your relationship have been set.

Chris and Maria Find Balance

Early in our marriage, Maria was consulting and making a good salary. We had no kids, plenty of security to pay bills, and the ability to save for the future. It was a low-stress time for us. Then Maria became burned out from all the travel her job demanded and decided to leave her consulting position to finish her MBA full time. This was a big adjustment for us. Not only did our income drop by half, our expenses went way up— business school is expensive! We agreed on a plan: once Maria graduated she'd pursue a career in marketing. Knowing she'd soon be out of school and undoubtedly doing well in that field was the light at the end of the tunnel for me. My job was secure, and my real estate investments with Todd were on solid ground. Still, I felt the weight of carrying us both acutely. But Maria was investing in her—and our—future, so we cut back on dinners out and travel and focused on getting to a more secure place in our lives.

As fate would have it, a month or two after Maria graduated, she became pregnant with our first child. Maria's pregnancy was a happy time for both of us, but a question simmered in the background during those nine months: after investing so much time and money in obtaining an MBA, would Maria seek work or stay home with our baby? If she stayed home, did that mean going back to school had been a waste? Was I ready to be the sole breadwinner for the foreseeable future? How could we find a work/life balance that made the most sense for our family? This was an ongoing conversation between us for months as we weighed the pros and cons for our family.

Ultimately, Maria chose to stay home and care for our now three children. We had to significantly cut back on leisure purchases and travel, and focus on allocating the appropriate funds for needs vs. wants in our lives. This was a challenging time for us: the stress and exhaustion of caring for babies can make arguments about money—or even whose turn it is to unload the dishwasher—seem catastrophic. As painful as it sometimes was (don't get me wrong: there was much joy in these early years, as well), we learned new things about each other. For example, I can now see Maria's desire to have a vacation we couldn't afford was really more about a *need* for family connection, not a *want* for an extravagant trip. She felt, at the time, my resistance to going was a form of control, of stinginess even, while my *need* is to feel safe, to make sure we have enough to keep our family afloat. Sometimes, you have to have the big fight to discover these fundamental character traits about your partner.

Ultimately, Maria and I made it through the baby years, the rough economy, and are now happy with how our family functions as a team. Before getting married and having children, we didn't fully understand how much would shift and how many compromises would be involved. But we have learned to shift together. And the shifts continue: once the kids got a bit older and were in school, Maria and I discussed her rejoining the workforce. Now she enjoys a job in marketing that increases our financial freedom. Nothing is forever: jobs change, careers pause, kids are born and grow up quickly. It's a wild ride made easier if you can communicate and support each other with trust and compassion. And while arguments about money are inevitable and often difficult, they are also illuminating. Try to look beneath the surface—you may discover a hidden truth about your partner.

Money and lifestyle: Not a One-Time Discussion

You'll notice that both our stories involve shifts after marriage in our imagined financial courses—and not just one shift, but several. What became clear to us is that while engaging in a deep discussion of your beliefs and desires around money *before* marriage is vital, *ongoing* financial discussions (not just "did you pay the electric bill?") are also essential. What's important financially when you're childless and just buying that first car together is very different than the issues you face when you're 45 and about to send three kids off to college in rapid succession.

Keeping the money conversation going as you grow and change is a key strategy in preventing hidden resentments from building up in your relationship. Shifts from co-breadwinners to one breadwinner, from working at home to working in an office, among others, can kick up all sorts of issues around how you and your spouse truly view each other's contributions to the family—financial and otherwise.

It's not necessarily important to have the same definition of work, you just have to be clear of what each other's definition of work is and be fine with it. For example, is work staying at home with the kids? Is having a full-time job that pays $100k per year more work than a full-time job that pays $25k? A great thing about marriage is you and your spouse get to divvy up household management, financial management, career management, and childcare however you both see fit. What's critical is that you both respect each other's efforts and unique challenges.

So how should you distribute the finances in your relationship? It really is whatever works best for your two personalities. One thing's for certain: expect a lot of people to think what works in their marriages should work for everyone! This is just not true. We see three general alternatives that seem to work well:

1) Keep it separate. Some couples, especially those who married after their careers were established, say not combining their money is their best option. In this scenario, couples often share expenses according to a proportion of relative incomes.

2) Combine some, not all. These couples often have a joint checking account for expenses like a shared mortgage, and keep personal accounts for their own spending outside of the household.

3) Everything's ours. In this scenario, couples consider all earnings "our" money and typically pool it into a single account.

These three approaches are as different as can be, and they'll all work—*if* the couple is on the same page. There is only one approach that seems to accelerate doom: If one spouse is hiding money or has an extra, secret bank account. That tells me the couple isn't talking about money to the point that trust has eroded.

Chris's Tips for Staying on Track

Although Maria and I regularly talk about our cash flow and spending, every year we pick a day to sit down and discuss the past year's financial performance. That involves looking at where we overspent, what unexpected costs popped up, and also where we saved.

I keep track of home expenses like utilities, taxes, television, cable, phones, etc. with the help of the latest accounting software. The program allows me to create reports and nice graphs with little effort. I consider this meeting my time to ensure Maria and I are on the same page regarding our financial position, and also to talk about projections for the coming year. Maria has a lot of confidence in me and typically trusts the financial decisions I make, but if she feels strongly about one thing or another she will voice her opinion and we make a mutually agreeable decision. That open communication and ability to find a compromise has been really important in our relationship.

Another way we stay on track is agreeing not to spend over a certain amount of money without informing the other. Many couples who don't have independent spending accounts agree on an amount above which they must consult the other before spending. As a single person, it was easy to head out and spend $100 on a pair of shoes or a night out. After all, you only had to justify the expense to yourself. Now, that money is shared by the two of you and may—in one person's mind—be allocated towards some other purchase. Whether it's $50 or $500, decide on the number together and then respect your agreement. Communication and trust: the key elements of staying on track.

Life Insurance: When and How Much?

Marriage is usually the life event that sparks the question: do I need a life insurance policy? This is especially true if you plan on having children. Too often, this task is put off or simply avoided altogether—one in four Americans currently have no life insurance at all.[11] But unless you are extremely wealthy—enough that, should you die, your current assets could support your family for years to come—we encourage you to obtain life insurance.

---

11   Epperson, Sharon. "How Much Life Insurance do you Need? CNBC, 10/5/14.

When deciding how much life insurance to procure, consider the following: what are your monthly expenses? How much income does your spouse bring in? How much is in your savings accounts? How many children will you be supporting? Do you plan on covering their college tuitions? Figuring out what you have versus what your family would need in your absence should bring you to the correct number. And keep in mind, you can make changes to your policy as your situation changes. Purchasing a life insurance policy may not be the most fun way to spend your money, but it is a safeguard against financial catastrophe as well as an expression of love.

• •

Money is a hot button issue in a marriage. Remember: it's not whether you disagree sometimes with your spouse that matters, but how you resolve it. If resolution seems unmanageable, try reaching out to therapists, clergy, trusted friends, or advisors—either with or without your spouse. Letting experts guide you and your spouse through a discussion of your finances could help you both learn the skills needed to communicate. If nothing else, read articles online or get books from the library on successful, calm, open communication.

Pearls of Wisdom

- Recognize that conflict around money is rarely about the money itself.

- Dig deep early to discover how you both approach financial matters.

- Embrace inevitable change and be flexible as your financial priorities shift over time.

- Decide the best way for you and your spouse to distribute your income(s).

- Communication is the key to resolving money conflict.

Chapter 5:
Giving Your Children the
Financial Skills They Need

*"It is not what you do for your
children, but what you have taught
them to do for themselves that will
make them successful human beings."*

– Ann Landers

As we have previously touched upon, how we
grow up heavily influences how we handle
our finances as adults. Whether our parents made
a conscious effort to demonstrate fiscal responsibility
or had a more casual attitude when it came to money,
they instilled in us the habits we now possess—or perhaps choose to reject. When we have children of our
own, it becomes our turn to carry the torch. We now
have the power to pass the financial skills that have
served us well in life on to the next generation. Since
our job as parents is ultimately to raise self-sufficient
adults, teaching them how to handle money is one of
the smartest—and *kindest*—things we can do to set

them on a path toward professional success and personal happiness.

Beyond simply forking over an allowance, instilling fiscal wisdom in your child is an act of love, a life skill akin to having good manners, eating right, and working hard—qualities that most parents make a conscious effort to impart. And, at least in the current state of our public schools, there are few opportunities to learn about personal finance in a classroom setting. The result: three out of four teenagers today lack the ability to understand the breakdown of a paystub.[12] Indeed, a recent poll found that 84% of high school students would *like* more education when it comes to handling money, but this subject is simply not included in most curricula.[13] It's up to us as parents to actually *be parents and raise our kids to understand money and how it impacts our everyday lives, rather than vainly hoping they'll pick up this knowledge elsewhere.*

Teaching Financial Savvy: There's No One Way To Do It

As is the case with most parenting quandaries, there is no one, slam-dunk way to raise financially responsible kids. This can either feel freeing or overwhelming. Wouldn't it be nice if there was a simple how-to guide you could follow and—voilà!—your kid works hard, saves his earnings, avoids bad debt, and invests wisely?

12   Kobliner, Beth. "Start Early to Raise Money-Savvy Kids" WSJ, 7/27/14.
13   Bortz, Daniel. "Why Most High Schoolers Don't Know How to Manage Their Money" US News & World Report. 10/9/12.

It's not so simple because people are not so simple: every child is different, and it's difficult to predict how external life events will mix with your child's personality.

What does that mean? Consider this: For every child who grows up in a lower-income home, feeling the fire in his belly to become wealthy, educated, and self-sufficient, there are many children who say growing up struggling and without good financial role models set them up for disaster. On the flip side, for every wealthy child whose family's money and connections helped him achieve a top-notch education and high-flying career, there are many who lean to the lazy side because they never needed to work growing up, or are irresponsible with money because they learned there was always more where that came from.

The good news: while there's no single way to raise children who are self-motivated and financially responsible, there are several parenting principles that we will explore that can shape your child—and they have nothing to do with household income.

From Diapers to Dollars

When is it appropriate to begin talking to your children about money? A generation or two ago, discussing financial matters with children was considered taboo. Times have changed. Most financial experts agree (and we concur) that introducing the subject of money to your preschool or kindergarten age child can set the stage for financial literacy. There are several lessons to impart at this tender age—and all sorts of online tools to assist you in your efforts. (We recommend *Don't Buy It*, a great website run by PBS kids: http://pbskids.org/dontbuyit/. It encourages kids to think critically about what advertisers and toy manufacturers are trying to sell them.)

Where to start? For our purposes, we will break it down into three categories: introducing the idea that items cost various amounts of money, that someone has to work to earn that money, and the bucket system. Children this young have little to no concept that their toys, toothpaste, bananas, and scooter all cost money. Begin by casually inserting this idea into your daily conversations with your preschooler. A simple trip to the grocery store can illustrate that each apple, box of raisins, or whatever food they enjoy, costs a certain amount of money. Every once in a while, pay cash and let them see you hand off dollars and coins to the cashier. For a kid, observing this transaction can transform money from a purely theoretical concept into a concrete thing you exchange for something you want.

Where does money come from? Kids see that on most days, daddy and/or mommy do some mysterious activity called "work." Explain to them what this means—that you perform your job for many reasons, but primarily in order to earn money to buy the items your family needs: food, clothing, and shelter. You can bring this idea home by giving your child a simple task such as cleaning up his blocks and pay him a nominal amount (see below for more on allowances). The key concept here is connecting the idea of work and money. The old saying "money doesn't grow on trees" still applies, and even if your kid receives birthday/holiday money in lieu of gifts, it's important to remind him of that connection.

Many of today's parents have adopted a pared-down 'bucket' system, less complicated than the one we discuss in Chapter 1. While there are many iterations of this, the basics are when a child either earns or is given money, he must divide it into three components: spend, save, and give. The exact percentage that goes into each bucket is up to you to decide (we suggest simply dividing the total into thirds) but this system instills early on the ideas of delayed gratification and charity, while still allowing the fun and learning experience of making consumer choices. From five-year-olds to grade-schoolers to teens, this is a system that can grow with your child. She may begin by saving for a toy and giving a few dollars to a homeless person and, down the road, decide to put money aside for a car and give to a charity they've researched online.

Todd: Colin Buys His First Car

Like most five-year-olds, my son Colin was enthusiastic about the toys that he desired. Teresa and I had been conscientious about instilling a sense of giving back and what things cost, so when Colin set his sights on a shiny new remote control car, he came to me with the birthday and chore money he had saved. We discussed how much the car cost, and how much more money he would need in order to purchase it. This was when he was first beginning to understand numbers, and I was pleased to be able to use this opportunity to nurture his budding math skills.

Even at five, Colin earned an allowance for cleaning the table after meals and emptying the forks and spoons from the dishwasher. It took him months to save up for the remote control car, but the day finally came when he had reached his goal. He came into the living room, piggy bank under his arm and a look of pride on his face. We went to the store to purchase the car, and he glowed with a special excitement as he handed over his hard-earned money to the clerk. As Colin grows, I continue to encourage him to think critically about his consumer choices and find that the very act of saving usually forces the issue of whether or not the desired item was worth it.

These are lessons that can be shared both at home and in your community. For instance, I'm currently organizing the junior achievement program at Colin's school, which teaches entrepreneurial skills and financial literacy (www.juniorachievement.org). Seek out your own such opportunities: volunteer-based organizations such as this can help fill the gaps, providing valuable knowledge missing from your child's curriculum. For our family and in our community, a philosophy of working hard for what you want is teaching our kids lessons that we hope set them up for a bright future.

The Allowance Debate

To give or not to give? Many parents of school-aged kids struggle with this dilemma, and we are no different. While six out of ten parents do hand over an allowance, the "deal" can look very different from family to family.[14] How much money is appropriate? Should they earn it through chores or simply receive it? What items should an allowance reasonably be expected to cover—clothes, toys, books, candy?

There are three main camps within the allowance debate. The first (to which Chris subscribes) holds that children should not be paid for doing the daily tasks that are expected of them. After all, no one pays *you for taking out the trash or doing laundry.* Insisting that your child contribute to the family by tackling simple chores such as keeping a tidy room instills a sense of teamwork and gratitude for everyone's efforts. Should he complete bigger, "extra" tasks such as walking the dog or washing the car, he may be rewarded with money or by non-monetary means such as extra screen time or doing some other enjoyable activity. If he needs money, he can use what he's saved from birthdays and holidays or simply ask for it.

On the opposite spectrum of the allowance debate (which Todd's family has adopted), kids receive an allowance if they complete a set of assigned chores. The thinking here is that children will make the

14 Barker, Joanne. "Children's Allowances: How Much is Enough?" WebMD, 2/29/12.

connection between work and money if they have to 'earn' it. Once they make their weekly pay, they still must divide it among the three buckets. An allowance is an opportunity to make money in a way that reflects adult life. With this in mind, consider deducting a "tax" from their gross amount, just like what happens with your own paycheck.

The third choice—a philosophy we wholeheartedly do not recommend—would be to simply set an amount of money your child automatically receives each week. Some families base this number on age (a dollar per year: your seven-year-old gets $7 a week) or by budget (based on what they need to buy and what their savings goals are). This scenario takes out the chore debate while also providing room for them to learn how to allocate and save. That said, some studies show that giving kids a regular, unconditional allowance does more harm than good, as it literally teaches kids that they can get money for nothing.

When it comes to an allowance, the most important thing is to be clear and consistent—this helps children learn to make plans for anticipated income. Once you agree upon the rules, there should be little negotiating. Choose the day of the week that your child receives his allowance and stick to it. That way, if he spends all his money at the beginning of the week and asks for more, he is introduced to an idea we're all accustomed to: waiting for payday.

Todd: Climb With Your Legs, Not Your Arms

As your children mature, the issues change, and there are ever more opportunities to observe and shape their fiscal behavior. By now, you know your kid's tendencies. Perhaps your daughter is a natural spendthrift who saves up for the items she wants, but your son's buddies have the latest tech gadgets and he can't resist splurging. It can be especially difficult as a tween or teen to have the maturity to resist wanting the latest clothes or games. One metaphor I have found useful for encouraging long-term planning over instant gratification is inspired by my love of rock climbing.

Like any sport, sometimes rock climbers like to talk about their accomplishments: I climbed this route with the tiniest of handholds or longest of overhangs. When I've focused on those times and numbers or otherwise gotten a bit overconfident on the rock, there's a temptation to pull myself up by my arms as fast as I can. I forget, in those moments of pride and competition that I'd actually climb more efficiently if I relied more on my legs.

Great climbers know their real power comes from their legs, which push them up the rock, rather than their upper bodies, which pull. They also know that over-using their arms will lead to becoming tired quickly, while relying more on the strength of their legs means they'll have the energy for a long, tough climb.

When you teach your children about your consumer choices, encourage them to climb with their legs. Climbing with your arms means you're doing what feels good in the moment but rarely serves you in the long run. For instance, buying the latest phone or trendy outfit just because that's what your friends—or worse—strangers on TV have. Climbing with your legs means tapping into your real strength—the strength that comes from planning, patience, and not worrying about the other guys.

These were values that I came by honestly. My parents are first-generation Americans. My mom's dad was a shoemaker and my dad's dad was a coal miner. Both came over from Italy at 18; they lived the classic story of immigrants coming to America without much money and working hard in low-paying skilled work just to scrape by. Having grown up with so little, and earning a very modest living themselves, my parents had no interest in raising kids who needed a bunch of 'stuff.' Other than the necessities like new shoes and school supplies, they very rarely bought me extra toys or treats unless it was my birthday or Christmas. There was no impulse purchasing at the store, even if I asked for something as simple as a candy bar. But here's where I was really fortunate: I never thought 'Oh, they must not love me because I didn't get that toy/candy bar/comic book.' I knew my parents loved me, period. The concept that money or material gifts would be used to show affection or prove love never entered my mind.

Material items can be exciting in the moment, but the thrill soon fades as we become accustomed to our bigger house or fancier car. Unwise consumer spending is, in reality, a byproduct of a deeper desire to feel good about ourselves (I'm just as cool as they are), even if the long-term impact will make us feel worse (I can't afford to retire). The credit card companies know this, which is why college campuses are riddled with their marketing voodoo. There are few reasons I can think of that a teenager or college student would need a credit card—a sure enticement to climb with their arms. A checking account attached to a debit card should be sufficient for managing the money they earn or is provided by you.

Now that you are a parent, you can ideally put a stop to the cycle of spend and regret. A crucial part of that is watching what you say—kids are keen observers, watchful for our habits and the messages they send. Sometimes climbing with your arms isn't just going to result in credit card debt; it also spreads the message of materialism and envy. Pay attention to the small things you say or do and see if you're sending your kids a hidden message. Do your kids hear you complain that so-and-so always gets to go on vacations? Do they see you give a regretful sigh when walking past Tiffany's at the mall? Do you talk about how you are happy now, or do you say happiness is something for "one day," if/ when the family has more money? Because my parents weren't buying me things that weren't necessities, I learned at a young age—about seven years old—that I still could get what I wanted; it'd just be up to me to earn the money and buy it myself.

Chris: Understanding Needs Versus Wants

Like Todd, I was raised in a middle class family that didn't have a lot of room for 'extras.' Given my dad's modest income, the concept of needs versus wants was a philosophy my parents lived by. They were constantly putting our family's needs first, and expecting me to, as well. New shoes versus a G.I. Joe figure? The debate wasn't really a debate at all. This clear understanding of prioritizing needs over wants hit home early and perhaps influenced my drive to work for what I wanted: at the age of ten, I began earning good money on a paper route. By the time we were in our teens, my landscaping business with Todd was bringing in several thousand dollars per year.

In a way, my income forced my parents into a "teachable moment," as we say these days. Every Sunday, I would collect the money I made and come home to find my dad at the kitchen table. I would hand over the envelope and watch as he divvied up my earnings, giving me an early education in priorities and budgeting. "Go grease your mother's palm," he would say. This was a sign of respect. My mom didn't work outside the home, but had the considerable job of managing it and raising my brother and me. I put the money next to her purse where she would find it. Next, I needed to pay the driver I used for my delivery route. From the remainder, my dad would set aside a good portion for my savings and the rest was mine—usually just a few dollars by that point. I didn't mind. Under his strict guidance, I learned the valuable lessons of taking care of the ones who take care of you.

This early lesson of money apportionment stuck with me and is something I consciously pass on to my kids. Today, each time they receive gift money from relatives, we sit down together and the ritual begins: they hand over their money, we split it evenly—half for the bank, half for discretionary spending—and Juliana or Nicholas fill out their respective deposit slips (since my youngest, Michael, is six I assist him in filling out the deposit slip). Then we head down to the bank together. Although it would be more convenient to simply hit an ATM, the act of handing over the cash to the teller and receiving the slip that shows their current balance answers their perpetual question: "Where does it go from here?" Having the balance in black and white on the receipt helps them realize their money is actually increasing in value as they receive interest on it. They are actively choosing to do the harder thing, to make the mature choice to set aside money that would be much more fun to spend on clothes or candy. Hopefully, this habit will become the solid ground upon which they build their financial literacy.

Real Life Tips for Raising a Financially Savvy Kid

The Do's

1) Talk about money. Look for chances big and small to be honest about what's financially possible for your family and what's not. Let middle-school kids see how much the weekly grocery store budget is and have them

help you shop. Start talking about college finances during high school.

2) Take your child to the bank, or at the very least let him or her hold a check before depositing it in the ATM, and then explain it's money and it's going into savings.

3) Discuss your consumer choices with your kid. If you drive a Honda Accord instead of a Lexus, make it clear you spend less on the car so your family can have money for other things.

4) Bring the children with you to the Goodwill, and explain some families aren't as fortunate so we share things we don't use anymore.

5) Encourage your children to seek out a job when they are teenagers, even if it's volunteering.

The Don'ts

1) Avoid being frivolous with your money—yes, even if you earned it and it's your right to do as you please with it.

2) Resist buying point of purchase items, like the tempting candy and magazines at the grocery store checkout. This sets an example that spontaneous purchasing decisions are routine.

3) Don't bail them out—it limits their own accountability around money. Allow your kids to work out their own financial problems. If you help them, their money missteps will only become bigger as they mature.

4) Many parents who both work try to make up for the lack of time they are around their children by buying them a lot of things. Unfortunately, this is the exact opposite of what kids need. Even 30 minutes of quality time a day is better than trying to "buy love."

5) Don't let them have everything they ask for.

. . . .

Encouraging financial literacy is an enormous gift—one you have the power to give no matter your current income level. We were lucky enough to have wise role models whose hard work and frugality we now emulate. (And, in today's crazed consumer culture, that is no mean feat!) By following the strategies above and embarking on your own quest for healthy financial habits, you can become the role model your children need to see.

Pearls of Wisdom

- Every child is different. Tailor your approach to fiscal education accordingly.

- It's never too early to begin talking to your kid about money.

- Teach your children to climb with their legs, not their arms.

- Discuss the concept of wants vs. needs early and often.

Suggested Reading

- *Little Critter: Just Saving My Money (My First I Can Read)* by Mercer Mayer

- http://pbskids.org/dontbuyit/

Chapter 6:
Home Ownership:
Still the American
Dream?

*"Real estate cannot be lost or stolen,
nor can it be carried away. Purchased
with common sense, paid for in full, and
managed with reasonable care, it is about
the safest investment in the world."*

– Franklin D. Roosevelt

With each stage of life, our notion of home changes. Up until this point, home may have been the house or houses in which you grew up, a dorm room, or a shared campus apartment. When we are young, we generally have little to no control over our living situation. Once launched into the world of work and income, however, a wide array of choices becomes available: do you prefer your own apartment, roommates, a house with a yard, a studio with a view? These options are constrained by income, job location, and relationship status, of course. But finally enjoying an active and independent say in where you live is a sought after freedom, indeed.

Before you go picking out paint colors and furniture shopping, a fundamental quandary will first present itself: do you rent or do you buy? This choice is one of the most important financial decisions you can make as an adult and depends on a multitude of factors, which we will discuss in detail below. Overall, the choice to either rent or buy should be approached with careful deliberation and a clear-eyed view of your long-term goals. Think of this decision as the launching point of your financial adulthood, a first step that can have far-reaching implications over the course of your life.

A Case for Home Ownership

Is home ownership still the American dream? We unabashedly say yes. The purchase of a home has long been viewed as something to aspire to, a bright bold beacon of success. Of course, our economy is in constant flux—recessions and boom times swing back and forth on a pendulum. But regardless of the overall economic climate, home ownership remains a symbol of prosperity.

Why buy? People purchase homes for all sorts of reasons, some of which are smarter than others. For us, there are three primary motivations for buying a home.

#1: Build Equity

First, you are building equity rather than throwing your money away on rent. Although renting can, in the short term, seem less daunting—Few up front costs! Not your problem when the furnace blows!—the sooner you begin building equity, the sooner you can realize key financial goals such as trading up for a dream house for your family or retiring comfortably. Though these aims may seem far off, you are in a prime position as a young person to enjoy the advantages that time affords you. Need more convincing? Many studies have demonstrated that, nationally, the cost of home ownership (including mortgage, insurance, taxes, and maintenance) can be up to 38 percent cheaper than the cost of renting.[15]

#2 Your Home is an Investment

Buying a home means more than simply acquiring a place to hang your hat—it is a strategic investment. As investments go, home ownership is a pretty safe bet. (We say this even after suffering through the 2008 crash!) History proves that over time, property in the U.S. increases in value: according to the National Association of Realtors, between 1993 and 2014, the median sales price of single-family homes grew 86%. Such appreciation should not be your primary purpose in buying a house or condo, especially if you plan on living there only a short while. The idea of an ever-

---

15   Prevost, Lisa. "Cheaper to Buy than to Rent." New York Times, 10/23/14.

increasing home value certainly makes this investment more attractive.

#3: A Mortgage-free Retirement

Finally, long term home ownership (not necessarily in the same house), can significantly increase your odds of a happy retirement. Of homeowners aged 70 and above, 30% have outstanding mortgages.[16] However, with careful planning, you can pay off your loan before you retire. Presto: a major monthly expense vanishes at the very moment you may need extra money to travel or for medical care.

• •

Beyond the above financial considerations, there are certainly psychological benefits to home ownership, a feeling of putting down roots and a sense of pride, not to mention the satisfaction of making a house your own by improving upon it or adding your own creative flair. While we acknowledge these facts, we are spreadsheet geeks at heart: when considering buying a home, your financial realities should carry more weight than any emotional pull you feel towards a specific property. Even given our enthusiasm for home buying, we've seen too many people make the mistake of purchasing more house than they could afford based on—you guessed it—emotions. Rather than focusing on the more transient satisfaction of material acquisition, consider

---

16 Hess, Alexander. "30-year mortgage, or 15? 5 questions to help you choose" USA Today, 11/7/13.

the deeper happiness you'll achieve if you purchase a home based on what you can afford. If you are smart with the numbers, you are more likely to feel a sense of security, pride, and long-term happiness.

So, You Want to Buy a Home

How do you know you're ready to take the leap into home ownership? The key factors here are time and stability of income. If you can be relatively certain that you will be staying in the same location for five years or more, buying may be a good bet. Consider the life you are currently living. Is your employment situation stable and, if not, could you find another job in the same city? Does the idea of putting down roots in your town put a smile on your face? Do you have a solid network of friends and family that give you a sense of belonging, a support system that makes committing to a place all the more attractive?

Moving on, how stable is your income? It's not so much the *amount that matters*. Rather, it's knowing that owning a home comes with ongoing and often unexpected costs. At the end of the day, buying can be cheaper than renting, especially if interest rates are low, but maintaining a property means you'll need cash-in-hand to fix the roof, the sink, the termite situation, or whatever inevitable upkeep the house needs. (Big-ticket maintenance items to look out for when you are shopping: the roof and the furnace. Even on a modest home, replacing these could be $5,000 to $10,000.) These costs mean that buying is more attractive if your employment situation provides steady and disposable income, as opposed to freelancing or living month-to-month.

The most common concern first time home buyers have is how to save for a down payment. Here's where we leave the rails of your typical home-buying advice. You are in a unique situation in your 20s. Unlike later in life when your responsibilities are likely to grow, you don't need a huge house in the expensive neighborhood with the good school district. Though your needs are modest, a savvy young professional knows that there is no time like the present to start building equity.

Still, that 20% down that everyone talks about is a lot of money, even for a starter home. Lucky for you, there are first time home buyer programs such as FHA loans that offer lower down payment options. We advise you put down as little as possible and always keep in mind the advantages of Other People's Money—or OPM, as we fondly call it. Whether it's the government, the bank, or your parents, seek ways to limit how much of your own cash you are putting towards a first home. We will discuss how to run the numbers to assess how much you can afford in the next section, but taking advantage of low interest and down payment offers can significantly lower your up front, out-of-pocket costs, increasing the chance of meeting your long-term fiscal goals.

Another advantage of buying a home in your twenties: roommates. Depending on the size of the house, a roommate or two or three is a great way to offset your monthly outlay, while all the while building equity in the home. This is likely one of the only times in your life you don't mind sharing a space with roommates—and you probably have single friends who would be happy to have you as a landlord. As your situation changes, you may want to purchase another home, while keeping your initial investment as a rental property.

You are at a critical juncture; taking these savvy steps toward responsible home ownership can launch you onto a path for fiscal success. This, of course, involves educating yourself, taking an honest view of your finances and prospects, and surrounding yourself with reliable realty and mortgage broker professionals. Oh, and did we mention the paperwork? Buying a home involves a gargantuan amount of paperwork. Consider yourself warned!

Chris Runs the Numbers: What Can You Afford?

When you are a renter, your landlord calls the shots, requesting a (hopefully) fair monthly rent. This number is set by the terms of your lease, though (and this is another disadvantage of renting) it may go up should you decide to renew. On the other hand, purchasing a property involves numerous variables that can significantly alter your monthly outlay, as well as the amount of interest you end up paying—and equity you end up building—at the end of the day.

At first glance, the complexity of these factors can seem intimidating. Have no fear! I am here to help. Figure #1 illustrates how you can use simple math to determine what your monthly payment will be, based on how much money you are able to put down. Once you understand this calculation, you can plug your own numbers into any number of online mortgage calculators such as bankrate.com to determine the best approach based on your budget and long term goals.

The scenarios presented below are based on the following loan assumptions: a term of 30 years at an interest rate of 6%. Keep in mind that your total monthly payment will also include property taxes and homeowners insurance which can vary widely depending on where you live. And, if you put less than 20% down, you may also have to pay Private Mortgage Insurance (PMI) that protects the bank should you default.

Fig. #1: Mortgage Payment Variables for 30-year Term at 6%

Purchase Price	Down Payment	Down Payment Amount	Prin. Amount of Mortgage	Mortgage Payment (Prin. + Interest)	Est. Taxes & Ins.	Total Monthly Payment
200,000	5%	$10,000	$190,000	$1,139	$325	$1,464
	10%	$20,000	$180,000	$1,079	$325	$1,404
	15%	$30,000	$170,000	$1,019	$325	$1,344
	20%	$40,000	$160,000	$959	$325	$1,284

As you can see, the higher the down payment, the lower your monthly cost will be. While at first glance this seems like a good thing—who wants more monthly expenses?—keep in mind that putting $40,000 down rather than $10,000 means that $30,000 that could be working for you elsewhere is now tied up in your home.

So what can you realistically afford? In order to achieve a workable number, many lenders maintain that your total PITI (Principle, Interest, Taxes and Insurance) should be no more than 28% of your gross income. The scenario below shows how this works:

Fig. #2: Example of PITI

Annual Income	Gross Monthly Income (annual/12)	Standard Lender Percentage	What you can afford (monthly income * .28)
$55,000	$4,583	28%	$1,283

Let's consider Figure #1 and Figure #2 together. If you are making $55,000 per year and interested in purchasing a home for $200,000, how much cash should you put down? According to these numbers, a 20% down payment will bring your monthly mortgage to an affordable amount, given your salary.

A Sucker's Game

Keep in mind, everything we've been discussing so far is based on an amortization of 30 years.

30-year mortgages are popular, encompassing 85% of new home loans.[17] It's easy to see why: the longer period of time means the monthly payments are lower, allowing people to buy more expensive houses. But we are here to let you in on a secret that the banks don't want you to know: 30-year loans are for suckers. Banks make their money on interest, and the longer the term of the loan, the more interest you pay. Although the monthly payment will obviously be higher, if you are able to purchase a 15-year property, you can build equity much quicker and cut your interest payments nearly in half. Figure #3 replicates the assumptions of Figure #1, but with a term of 15 years rather than 30.

Fig. #3: Mortgage Payment Variables for 15-year Term at 6%

Purchase Price	Down Payment	Down Payment Amount	Prin. Amount of Mortgage	Mortgage Payment (Prin.+ Interest)	Estimated Taxes & Insurance	Total Monthly Payment
200,000	5%	$10,000	$190,000	$1,603	$325	$1,928
	10%	$20,000	$180,000	$1,519	$325	$1,844
	15%	$30,000	$170,000	$1,435	$325	$1,760
	20%	$40,000	$160,000	$1,350	$325	$1,675

17   Frankel, Matthew. "Why Aren't 15-Year Mortgage Rates More Popular?" The Motley Fool, 7/29/14.

Fig. #4: Comparison of 15 and 30 year loans at end of term

Loan Amount	Loan Term	Mortgage Payment (Principle + Interest)	Number of payments	Total amount of Payments	Total Interest Paid
$170,000	15	$1,435	180	$258,220	$88,220
	30	$1,019	360	$366,925	$196,925

Here's where things get interesting. Working from Figures #1 and #3, let's say you put down 15%, borrowing $170,000 from the bank. Once the term of your 30-year loan is up, you've forked over $196,925 in interest payments. Contrast this to the total interest you would pay on a 15-year loan: $88,220. Looking at Figure #4 above, it's easy to see why, if you can do it, taking on a more onerous monthly mortgage expense pays off hugely down the road. In this scenario, choosing the shorter loan period means saving $108,705 in interest payments! Even if you had been disciplined enough to invest your money rather than pay down your mortgage more quickly, a guaranteed 6% return would be a pretty tough find.

Figure #5: Principle Balance Comparison after 5.5 years.

Loan Amount	Loan Term	Down Payment	Years Passed	Principle Balance
$200,000	15	0% ($0)	5.5	$146,382
$160,000	30	20% ($40,000)	5.5	$147,582

*Here's another calculation that may surprise you, illustrated in Figure #5: if you put down 20% on a 30-year loan versus 0% down on a 15-year loan, the mortgage balances will be the same after five-*and-a-half years (i.e. they both have the same amount of equity). In addition, the 15-year loan is completely paid off in half the time. Signing up for a shorter loan period takes discipline. Though it makes definite financial sense in the long term, be sure you have enough stability (including maintaining a solid emergency fund) to make it work. If you don't feel comfortable with a more aggressive approach, you may be better served by taking on lower and longer monthly payments.

When Renting Makes More Sense

Sure, we tend to get excited when it comes to investing in real estate—whether it's a moneymaking effort or personal residence. But we heartily admit that buying a home is not for everyone. Are you someone who longs for change and travel? Is there a decent chance your employer will ask you to relocate in the next few years? In such cases, renting allows flexibility and freedom—not to mention avoiding the significant costs of maintenance, closing fees, professional services, insurance, and property taxes that home ownership requires.

The smart renter recognizes that, although there is money saved by avoiding up front costs and having to replace a heating and air conditioning unit, he or she is not currently developing any equity. Is there a good way to offset this fact? Though it demands discipline, the savvy choice would be to take the money presumably saved in the short term by renting and invest it wisely. To wit: between 1983 and 2013 home values have increased at a rate of 3.6% per year; during the same period the compound annual return on the S&P 500 was 11.1%.[18] Allowing this money to grow can help you jump on the path to home ownership should your life become more stable down the road.

Todd Takes the Long View

In my many and varied real estate ventures, I have purchased houses, condos, and duplexes. Some I lived in and some I rented out, but in each instance, the numbers had to make sense. I'd ask myself—does this investment line up with my goals? Based on my current income, can I really afford this? Interestingly, my family has never resided in any property I have purchased—Teresa bought the home we live in now before we were married. In fact, my wife is a great example of how to leverage a modest first home purchase into a family home. When she was in her 20s and living in Houston, Texas, Teresa put down 5% on a 30-year loan and bought a house for $160,000. The property was in a rather seedy, yet up-and-coming neighborhood (a strategy that can really work when you are young), and four years later she sold it for a profit of $40,000. By this time, she and I were seriously dating, so she moved to Charlotte. Teresa

18   Andriotis, Annamaria. "The New Math of Renting vs. Buying." WSJ, 5/2/14.

again put down 5% for an interest only ARM loan at a rate of 3.75% and paid $185,000 for the home in which we currently live on Woodruff Place. As interest rates came down, we refinanced into a 15-year loan, and then recently into a 10-year loan. We plan to make extra payments as our finances allow in hopes of this house being paid off in seven or eight years.

With a careful eye on interest rate fluctuation and keeping in mind the money saved avoiding long term loans, Teresa's savvy choices have set us up for our next move. Today, we are considering adding on to and remodeling one of the investment properties that I purchased in 2004 and living there. I bought this modest house on Grandin Road in a neighborhood that I felt would appreciate with this very idea in mind—a place to really settle down and stay for a long while. At the time, I paid $150,000 on a 30-year loan so the rent would cover the low mortgage payments. Today, this property would likely be valued around $250,000.

Looking forward, our goal with the house on Grandin Road is to have a payment of $2,000 per month that we will pay off in 15 years, which will put me at 58 years old, right in line with my goals. How will we get there? I originally paid $150,000, and the cost of the renovation will be another $150,000. Given that there will be some built-in equity, I'll take out a 15-year loan for $300,000 at the current rate of 3.25% (vs. a 4% rate for a 30-year loan). This brings our payment to $2,100 a month, which is within 5% tolerance of my $2,000 budget, so I'm fine with that. Plus, we plan on turning the house on Woodruff into a rental property, which will provide us with additional income to either invest or pay off our Grandin loan sooner.

My goal with this property, of course, is to provide stability for my family. Growing up, I lived in the same home on the same street for the first 21 years of my life. I want my children to have that same stability and nostalgia for their childhood home. But my other consideration has to do with my retirement. I'm approaching this property with an eye towards the future: I will work the numbers so that this loan is paid off by the time I am 60. It is incredibly important to me that I am free and clear of mortgage debt once I stop working. And, because I know the advantages of taking out shorter term loans, I will make this happen for my family.

⚬ ⚬

Deciding to rent or buy a home requires a solid grasp of your current situation as well as your goals for the future. The choice should not be made casually. Once you look at the numbers and understand how to work the variables, hopefully you will be able to purchase a property that fits your life. Investing in a home should be part of your plan for now or the near future, and we hope you can get going on that future as soon as possible.

Pearls of Wisdom

- If you can, buy a starter home.

- Consider roommates to help defer your monthly costs.

- Take a clear-eyed view of what you can afford based on numbers, not emotions.

- Buying property isn't for everyone: if you're likely to move or your income is unstable, renting may make more sense.

- When you buy, have your retirement goals in mind.

Part III: Business Smarts

For many of us, the pursuit of a career is a primary focus in our lives. It provides us with stability, a sense of pride, a skillset, and—crucially—income. Whether you're climbing the corporate ladder, launching a startup, or building a real estate empire, your career choices will have longstanding repercussions. This section will discuss the smart strategies that can help you achieve your goals—and shine a light on the potential blunders that can set you off course.

Chapter 7:
Choosing a Career

"And will you succeed?
Yes! You will, indeed!
(98 and 3/4 percent guaranteed.)"

– Dr. Seuss

Your career may be a long and winding road, a straight shot up to the corner office, or a journey that zigzags as your interests and skills shift along the way. As you envision what you want to do for work, you'll have a much more enjoyable life if you feel a sense of excitement and purpose. After all, choosing a career is about much more than simply receiving a paycheck; it's about your passion, your dreams. You're at the beginning of a journey with plenty of unknowns, but with thoughtful planning, you can discover and do what you love for a lifetime.

And, when we say lifetime, we mean it. Think about it: you will likely spend the majority of your waking hours doing whatever your chosen profession is. According to the Bureau of Labor Statistics, employed people between the ages of 25 and 54 spend an average of 8.7

hours per day at work, 7.7 hours sleeping, 2.5 hours on leisure activities, and 1.3 hours caring for others.[19] Why spend most of your hours doing an activity that you don't particularly enjoy or—worse—actively hate? Life is too short for a career that is anything other than one you love.

Where Do You Start?

Choosing a career path can seem daunting. For this reason, it's never too early to begin soul searching about what it is that you love to do. The purpose of high school and college is, of course, to learn certain skills and key facts. But when it comes to launching a career, a solid education provides an even more crucial foundation: it gives you exposure to many different disciplines so you can hone in on what you enjoy and what you are good at. A freshman course in biology may spark an interest that inspires a career in the sciences or medicine. In Spanish class you may realize you have a great aptitude for foreign languages, which could lead to any number of fields. Extracurricular activities can also provide clues: you would never have realized your passion for set design had you not helped out with the school play. For us, our early experiences launching our landscaping business and real estate ventures fostered a lifelong interest in business and real estate.

Take advantage of your school's career counselor who may have practical advice and aptitude/personality

---

19   Charts from the American Time Use Survey, US Dept of Labor, 9/30/14. http://www.bls.gov/tus/charts/

tests that can confirm your propensity for a certain livelihood. (One key point is to answer the questions on such assessments honestly. These tests are pretty accurate to the data provided and only helpful if they are a true mirror of your tendencies and interests.)

We also advise seeking out a mentor once you have chosen a major. This person can be invaluable in understanding what your options are with a certain major. He may also suggest a different route, if it seems your skills and interests aren't exactly in line with your current field of study. Keep in mind, a mentor doesn't necessarily have to be a professor. Consider knowledgeable people from jobs you have held, friends of your parents, or folks in the community whose interests align with yours.

This is no time to be shy. Most people remember what it was like to be young and exploring their options and are happy to advise you. Many will have fond memories of their own mentors, who helped them gain a first foothold in their chosen careers. Begin by asking for a brief meeting to see if you have the right chemistry. If appropriate, see if there is an opportunity to shadow your mentor at his place of business—you may think being a chef is a great idea, but discover you hate being in a commercial kitchen all day. There's no substitute for actually witnessing the day-to-day realities of a specific job.

Is Graduate School for You?

For most people, graduating college means heading out into the real world with a bachelor's degree and a smile. But at some point along the way, you may feel the pull to pursue an advanced degree. And in some cases, this is an excellent choice—if you are interested in a career that requires graduate school, such as medicine, or if you want to become a professor; if you are in a highly competitive field (high finance, for instance) and getting an MBA will make you stand out among your peers; or if you are simply hungry for a certain body of knowledge and have surplus money and time in which to become an expert at it.

Graduate school can be a gigantic waste of time and money, however, if it is approached out of fear, boredom, or because someone other than yourself *really, really wants you to become a lawyer*. Think about it: those years spent studying (and likely taking on more student loans) could have been spent on the job learning, getting raises, and rising through the ranks. According to *Forbes magazine, you can assume every dollar of debt will cost two dollars by the time you pay it back*. Will a graduate degree ensure your salary will be sufficient to cover such a liability? If you are on the fence regarding whether or not to apply to graduate school, be sure to ask for advice from several people in your chosen field. Their paths to their current positions may surprise you.

Assessing Career Risk

There is no better time than when you are young to take a risk on a career path. Every chance you take provides you with new knowledge about the world and, most importantly, about yourself. At this point, you likely don't have a family to support or a mortgage to pay. If you want to give Hollywood a try for a few years and see if you make it as an actor, there is no time like the present. If you have a grand and risky business idea you want to tackle, go for it. (See Chapter 10 for our own grand and risky Hungarian wine enterprise. Lots of lessons learned— the hard way!) When you are older and have more responsibility, taking such risks becomes more difficult. But now, you may very well succeed, or, if your dream doesn't quite work out the way you had hoped, you are not going to be in that much of a worse position than when you were just out of school. The worst possibility is looking back and regretting that you never took a chance.

Every pursuit—whether you want to become a rock star or a banker—has inherent risks. And the truth is, the way you envision a certain job will be vastly different than the reality of it. That's why we say, have a solid plan, pursue your dream, and if it doesn't work out, alter that dream to something more accessible. In our experience, the most successful people are doing something they are passionate about. How they get there may have involved different paths, however. You may have to take a job you don't love for a few years in order to save up enough capital to start your dream business. Perhaps you pursue your passion part time while your full time job pays the bills until you are in a position to devote yourself fully to your dream. Maybe you've got two part time jobs while you get the graduate degree necessary to pursue your passion. The important thing to keep in mind is to keep your eyes on the goal of pursuing a career you love.

The First Job Blues: Todd Becomes a Banker

A first job out of college can be a leap of faith. Will you enjoy your chosen field now that it's more than a concept, when you have to wake up each day and actively practice it? Will you like the people? The atmosphere? Starting any new career will be full of unknowns and surprises, both good and bad. Your first job may not be your dream job, but I'll bet it holds a treasure chest of life lessons.

When I graduated from college, I headed straight into a three-year corporate banking training program. I was thrilled. This would be my fast track up the ladder into the lofty world of high finance. Or would it? As I looked around during those first months, I soon realized there was no way I wanted to spend the next 20 years being a commercial lender. The work was tedious and didn't inspire me. But instead of berating myself for a career misstep, I noticed there were opportunities in my position to focus on the elements of the job that *did interest me*. For example, learning how to analyze the financial condition of a company is an invaluable tool that I knew could be applied to any number of different positions in the future, not least of which would be running my own business.

Within the daily grind were bright spots I took it upon myself to pursue and amplify. I didn't care for writing detailed financial reports about the companies I was analyzing for the bank, but I did enjoy meeting with the business owners and learning their stories. As often as possible, I put myself in the position to go out on business calls with the lender to meet the owners and financial officers of these companies. I also knew that I was passionate about real estate investing. So every chance I got, I volunteered to work on the credit reports for the bank's real estate clients and learn as much as I could about analyzing real estate deals.

This first job was not a perfect fit for me, and that was okay. The skills I acquired at the bank are some I still use to this day. Some positions you will have along your career journey will be a bit skewed—you'll find the work boring or the personality of the place doesn't suit you. In such a situation, glean what skills you can, and when the time is right prepare to move on. You're not alone: according to the *Wall Street Journal, half of those employed between the ages of 20 and 24 have been in their current positions less than a year.*[20] The worst-case scenario: you are learning what type of job you *don't enjoy.* This is crucial information, not to be underestimated! It will help you to recognize and seek

---

20   The Numbers Guy. "Seven Careers in a Lifetime? Think Twice, Researchers Say" WSJ, 9/4/10.

out those positions that can become the jewels in your career crown.

Course Correction

Imagine you're a marketing major who got a great job with a great company right out of school and now... you dread going to work every day. Or you're in your second year of law school and realize you're in it for all the wrong reasons. It's not too late to course correct and choose a different path. No doubt, the younger you are when you decide to jump ship and pursue another dream, the easier it will be. But people make mistakes, change, or their interests shift over time. Having the courage to begin something new is wiser than white knuckling your way through a career you don't enjoy. And for today's youth, finding happiness in a job is critical: according to one survey of Generation Y workers, "88% consider 'positive culture' important or essential to their dream job, and 86% said the same for work they found 'interesting.'"[21]

The marketing major starting her own line of handmade jewelry or the would-be lawyer switching to social work because it inspires him are success stories. That said, some course corrections do not end happily, and this usually has something to do with your inner compass going haywire. If you find yourself hopping from career to career to career step back and be straight with yourself about the real reasons you might be changing

21   Meister, Jeanne. "Job Hopping Is the 'New Normal' for Millennials: Three Ways to Prevent a Human Resource Nightmare" Forbes, 8/14/12.

interests so often. An inability to settle into any field of interest could be a sign of some deeper issues you need to address.

When It's Time to Move On: Chris Makes a Tough Call

There comes a point in every job where you've learned all there is to learn or advanced as far as you're going to advance. Choosing to pursue a new job should involve careful consideration, and it can often be a great thing for your overall career. Today's worker stays at a job an average of 4.4 years.[22] So, approaching my 15th anniversary at a family-owned real estate firm, my staying power was off the charts.

There were a number of reasons I had remained there so long. The owners of the family-run company treated me like family. I had plenty of responsibility and the freedom to work the way I like to work—nurturing relationships and closing deals. Every two or three years, my responsibilities grew, which kept me interested and feeling challenged. But as time passed, I could feel myself stagnating. More critically, though management treated me as one of their own, the fact was I wasn't family. As I watched the third generation of future owners graduate and come aboard, I realized that my knowledge and experience far exceeded theirs, but someday they would be my bosses. This was quite

---

22   Meister, Jeanne. "Job Hopping Is the 'New Normal' for Millennials: Three Ways to Prevent a Human Resource Nightmare" Forbes, 8/14/12.

an uncomfortable epiphany as I looked down the line to 15-20 more years of work.

For a while, my dissatisfaction simmered on the back burner; it was easy to ignore my restlessness as I felt grateful for my comfortable position that paid me well. Then, an unanticipated opportunity presented itself that I could not discount. A long-time business associate from a local bank asked me out to lunch to discuss a position that had recently opened up in their real estate division. At first, I felt disloyal even to consider it. The firm had been so good to me, after all. This was clearly going to be an emotional decision as well as a pragmatic one, the biggest career move of my life.

I ran through the list of pros and cons for each alternative, and on paper the new opportunity proved superior. My decision-making process took into account the practicalities such as pay and benefits and growth opportunities. But I also took time to reflect on who I am and what I need.

My current company was comfortable, for sure, and I felt appreciated there, but what I needed more than security was new opportunities that challenged me and provided steady growth. There wasn't much opportunity for that in my current position. It was time to move on.

When you feel the itch that it may be time to leave one job for another, careful consideration is in order. Why do you suspect it's time to go? Legitimate reasons include a sense of boredom, a lack of feeling challenged, or a limited opportunity for pay/responsibility increases. Are you procrastinating, approaching your projects with less enthusiasm, taking longer and longer showers in the morning? These may be signs to begin polishing your resume.

That said, not everyone likes change or desires ever-increasing challenges. Some of us are happy to settle into a comfortable position and remain there doing great work and feeling secure. It's often the case that low stress, flexible jobs are a good match for those who are balancing caretaker demands at home. Understanding yourself and what you need will require you to take a deeper look inside. If you uncover what makes you happy—and this may be in defiance of what others expect—you'll be more likely to successfully navigate your career.

"You're Hired!"

Whether it's your first job or your fifth, they all begin the same way—with an interview. In order to be a strong candidate, of course dress presentably and be prompt. Just as important: do your research beforehand. Understand the company and the business they practice; anticipate the questions they may ask and have ready answers to how your strengths may be a great fit for their company. Your research should uncover the possible levels of pay, so know what you want (and what you can live with) before the interview. Bottom line: If you come across as understanding the business and what drives the bottom line, an employer is more likely to pay you a higher salary. This is also a way to justify the salary you are requesting if it is a little higher than the employer may originally want to pay.

Note: it is always preferable to seek out new employment while you are currently working. Not only do potential employers prefer to hire those who are employed, you'll feel more confident and be in a better position to negotiate your starting package. If, on the other hand, you walk into the interview unemployed it can raise uncomfortable questions and any leverage you had disappears. Plus, if you don't get the job, you can always fall back on your current employment and not worry about how you're going to pay your bills.

On the Job Tips

There are some truisms that apply to the working world whether you are a doctor, teacher, or dolphin trainer. They are simple and universal and if you apply them to your career, you'll likely succeed.

1) *Do your job and do it well*

   While this may seem obvious, it is often the case that a new hire comes aboard on fire to do great work and then, over time, plateaus into just getting by. Don't let this happen to you. Approach your work with continued passion, always striving for better results. In this way, promotions and raises will surely follow.

2) *Produce more than you consume*

Be an asset to your company—not a liability. Whatever it is your job to create—whether it's money or internal organization or beautiful letterhead design—keep it coming. Your employer will be more likely to reward those who can show concrete results rather than those who come in each day with not much to show for it.

3) *Beware social media*

Whatever social media outlet you use, just assume that your employer will see its contents. Privacy on the internet is a fallacy, so if you post something questionable, there is a good chance someone whose respect you value may take note. Keep party pictures and the like in a photo album at home or on your private hard drive instead.

4) *Avoid office gossip*

Professionalism means staying above the fray when it comes to office gossip. While it may be tempting to create alliances this way, the innate negativity of this kind of chatter is usually demeaning to someone and always an unnecessary distraction. Create friendships at work based on shared interests, personal connection, and positive communication.

5) *Be yourself and enjoy it*

Don't get wrapped up in trying to be the boss's favorite or saying things because you think it's the "right thing to say." If you are employed in an environment where you feel you continually have to wear a mask, hiding your true self, the job probably isn't a good fit. Perhaps it's time to look for the next, better, opportunity.

· ·

Your career will be a key centerpiece of your life. Down the road, will you look back at the choices you made and be satisfied? Yes, if you approach each step with deliberate, thoughtful intention. Your career path should reflect not only your needs (salary, retirement security, pride), but also your values. What do you love? What is important to you? What do you want to give to the world? If you ask yourself these questions during each career transition—from choosing a major to finding a first job to every job after that—you will end up creating the career of your dreams.

Pearls of Wisdom

- Begin noting early on where your interests lie.
- Find a mentor to help guide you.
- Seek a career that reflects your passion.
- Learn from every opportunity—even the jobs you don't love.
- Know when it's time to move on.

Chapter 8:
Business Relationships:
What is Your Gut
Telling You?

*"Coming together is a beginning;
keeping together is progress;
working together is success."*

– Henry Ford

We've spent much of this book exploring how our emotions can bubble up in strange ways regarding money, usually to our disadvantage. There's one big exception to this, and that's your gut feeling. When deciding to develop a business relationship with someone. That person could be a tenant for a rental property, a financial adviser, or, more significantly, a partner in a new business venture or investment opportunity.

For some people, gut feelings or intuition seem mysterious and all too easy to disregard. Sure, sometimes it can be wiser to rely on hard evidence and numbers.

But your gut is a tool that can be strengthened to help you make your best and ultimately soundest decisions with money and business. According to neuroscientist Antonio Damasio of the University of Southern California, gut feelings are signals from the insula and amygdala areas of the brain. They are sensations that tell you if whatever you are experiencing—a person, job opportunity, apartment, etc.—"feels" right...or seems a bit off. By paying attention to these messages—sometimes subtle, but often persistent—we can guide our decision making process toward the best path.[23]

Chris on Trust in Business

In the age of social media, I know I'm not alone in feeling like a lot of personal interaction between people has been lost. That doesn't mean we should give in or give up, though. The simple truth is it's hard to get the sense of what a person is really like online, and no technology is going to change that. Body movement and posture, facial expressions and conversation tone—these things all reveal more than 100 tweets ever will.

I sound like my father grumbling about 'kids these days,' but I think it's true: while the Internet is a fantastic tool in many ways, it is no replacement for true human interaction. For me, developing my sense of someone is always going to mean meeting in person, or at the very least, talking on the phone. I can't develop an opinion solely on email or technology. In most instances, I can determine from the first face-to-

23   Goleman, Daniel. "The Focused Leader." HBR, 12/13.

face meeting if someone is a person with whom I'd feel comfortable doing business. If you're the same way, don't feel apologetic about pushing for more in-person interaction.

Once I've met with a potential investment partner and feel comfortable with him or her, the next step is to ask myself if this person sees the 'deal' the same as I do and vice versa, as this is definitely a two-way street. Are you both in sync as far as strategy goes? Do you agree on the long-term goals? And how can each of you exit the investment if necessary? By asking these key questions up front you can avoid future misunderstandings and wasted time .

Other qualities I look for in a potential partner:

- Same desire and drive as me
- Financial capabilities
- Ethical decision-making
- Someone who balances out my weaknesses and vice versa

It's also smart to develop a circle of people you truly trust and respect, so you can ask them for recommendations and second opinions. That circle doesn't have to be big—it's often better if it's not, actually.

My circle, of course, includes Todd. We always seem to be on the same page at heart, yet we see things differently, and I mean that in a good way. Because there is mutual respect and trust, hearing Todd's view when it's a bit different from mine is refreshing. We've also built on the ability to find a solution or compromise we're both comfortable with, and that certainly is a characteristic that all long-term relationships need to survive, business or otherwise. That trust did have a funny consequence for us once. Todd saw a condo in Charlotte he really liked. I was in Ohio and unable to look at the condo in person, but I saw the numbers, and the numbers worked. Otherwise, I never would have bought property without seeing it. Well, next time I was in Charlotte, I saw the condo—and I didn't like it! I thought the view was bad. But Todd was the one who really knew Charlotte, and my trust in him was well-placed. We still own that condo today and it makes money for us. It's funny because now I love that condo.

Remember that as long as you keep learning, your intuition will become more useful and accurate. I probably would not be able to give advice about how to sense who to work with or what business ventures to pursue 15-20 years ago. I was just developing my own skills in real estate and learning the business, and sometimes you really just have to learn through repeat first-hand experience when to trust your instincts about business partnerships. Actually, the research supports this. An important 2008 study on intuition from professors at Leeds University Business School in the United Kingdom found that gut instinct is best used when accompanied by extensive knowledge on the subject—in this case, dealing with people, a skill that only comes with experience. Massimo Pigliucci, a philosophy professor at City University of New York, concurs: "Intuition is the result of your subconscious brain picking up on clues and hints and calculating the situation for you, and that's based solely on experience."[24] So, you can look back on the business partner who seemed a great fit when you were 25 and see why it didn't work out now that you are 40. Ah, the power of hindsight. But it's all good news: with each misstep comes the experience that strengthens our intuition. It's a tool that grows with time.

Todd on Trust in Business

If I'm deciding whether to work with a certain CPA or attorney, a lot of my decision will be based on the person's professional style and philosophy. Almost everyone likes to work with people who are similar to themselves, and I'm no different. Although my choices are ultimately about business first and foremost, I still like to ask myself: Is this someone that I would want to just hang out with or enjoy talking to at lunch? That helps me weigh what a person is like as a whole, and whether I think they're down to earth, a quality that happens to be important to me. You may have your own list of characteristics that appeal to you in a potential business associate: a sense of seriousness, a certain level of educational achievement, an extrovert or an introvert—everyone has different needs. The key is finding a match that is mutually advantageous.

---

24   Barton, Eric. "Trusting Your Gut: Smart Management or a Fool's Errand?" BBC Capital, 9/24/13.

There are a few go-to people that I will run things by just to get a second opinion. Those people include my brother Lance, Chris, and my wife, Teresa. Depending on the specific financial matter, I'll also consult with other people that I consider financially smart and conservative. I also tend to go back to "the numbers." If the numbers don't work then I don't make the investment, purchase, etc. This is usually a good reality check when my emotions start to get the best of me. So, yes, I do rely on intuition when seeking a business partner, but I also ensure through trusted advice and hard facts that my instinct is on the right track. It's a balancing act that is different for each of us.

Trust can also sometimes mean paying more, and I'm fine with that. Our current property manager is 15 percent more expensive than our previous one, but we don't have late payments of rent and he is responsive to our calls and questions. The scanner in my office? I probably could have gotten it a bit cheaper on the web at a discount online site, but a mom and pop store out of Denver provided me such exceptional service over the phone that I went with him. When my scanner arrived and he even helped me set it up, I later spent a little extra to buy a printer from him because the service was worth it to me and I respected his efforts. Of course, opting for the good salesman at Best Buy is not as significant a venture as, say, hiring the right employee or choosing the best CPA for your needs. But the lesson remains: often you get what you pay for.

While I appreciate all that money can do for me, I'm not personally into a lot of material flash, so someone who lives in a house they can't really afford or who drives a fancy car and needs to mention often how important they are, well, it turns me off from doing business with them. It's just not who I am. I've always felt it's important to just be who you are, and a great thing about aging is that you should feel more and more liberated to just be yourself, and feel less of a need to justify your choices, including walking away from a deal or a person who just isn't a good fit. No one can please everyone so don't even try.

The people I trust most when it comes to a joint investment are Chris and my brother. These are people I have known my entire life and trust implicitly. There are so many different things that can go wrong in a business deal and disagreements can come up; it is very difficult to know how someone will react without having seen them deal with different types of pressures and stress in the past. Despite the oft-repeated success stories—Google's Larry Page and Sergey Brin, Bill Hewlett and Dave Packard, Ben and Jerry—more than half of all business partnerships end in failure.[25]When I first moved to Charlotte in 2000, I reached out to an old friend from grade school. Dan had lived in town for many years, so was familiar with the home values in various neighborhoods. At first glance, he was just the kind of partner I needed: I was hungry to buy an investment property and here was someone with local expertise. We decided to purchase a home in Eastover, one of the most desirable neighborhoods in Charlotte, and rent out rooms to cover the mortgage.

25 "How to Make Partnership Work." Small Biz Viewpoints, 5/19/10.

Dan would be the only name on the loan and carry a larger percentage of the mortgage, so this looked like a solid deal. With only a handshake (my first mistake), I was now responsible for $1,000 a month—a hefty sum, as I was just starting out as a financial adviser. We took the roommate approach for a few years before my doubts about the wisdom of this purchase began to surface. On a more modest property, I could have been paying a lot less per month and building equity. But this house was a monster, and it was hurting me financially every month. Besides, it wasn't as if I would ever own it outright.

I began to realize that Dan and I had wanted something very different from this property from the start. I had seen it as an investment that we would either sell or fully rent out and cash flow; to him, it was a status symbol, one in which he eventually wanted to live. Which is exactly what happened—I got out of the deal and he still lives there to this day. So why did I enter into this time-waster of a partnership if we had such a misalignment of goals?

First, I got caught up in the potential appreciation of this house because of the "old money" neighborhood. I knew Charlotte was a hot market and didn't want to miss out on a good opportunity. Second, and most crucially, I avoided working out the details of the deal with Dan simply because I was afraid we never would have come to an agreement. I kept telling myself, "Oh, things will just work out." I was overly optimistic, never really discussing with him up front how exactly we would each make our money. Emotions got the best of me as I ignored the potential downsides. Lesson here: Don't avoid working out the details of a deal with your potential partner out of fear that it may fall apart—often that can be the best case scenario.

There is a time and place for emotions, but as I learned from the Eastover property, becoming emotionally attached to an investment can cloud your decision-making. Now, when I notice someone getting too emotionally attached to an investment—whether it is a house, a stock, or simply purchasing a car—I tend to run the other direction when it comes to partnering with him or her. Of course, every successful investor ends up doing this a time or two over the course of a career, but there are some people to whom investing with their emotions is the norm, as opposed to relying on hard facts and analysis. This person is probably not a wise fit.

• •

A final consideration when seeking the right partner is noticing whether you share the same philosophy when it comes to investing. Are you a risk-taker, or do you tend to be more frugal? Are you cautious and detail-oriented when making an investment, or do you like to throw yourself into a project? For me, one of my philosophies is that you make your money at the beginning of the deal. An easy example is buying real estate at a discount (when the value is depressed for one reason or another) as opposed to counting on the appreciation.

This could also apply to investing in the stock market. Out of all of my clients, there are only one or two that were excited when the market dropped by 50%. The reason they were excited is because the market all of a sudden had become a great "value"—a once in a lifetime opportunity. If you listened to people like Warren Buffet or watched how he capitalized on opportunities during the Great Recession, it is easy to see why he is a successful investor. These people operate above fear and can tune out the noise of everyone panicking. Finding someone whose financial philosophy is similar to yours can make for a beautiful partnership; a misalignment can be an expensive waste of time.

Pearls of Wisdom

- Listen to your gut, which gets wiser with age and experience.

- Face-to-face interaction is priceless.

- Have a go-to circle of trusted advisers for second opinions.

- Know yourself: What characteristics are important to you in a partner?

- Don't be afraid to dissolve a non-workable partnership.

Chapter 9:
Real Estate Investing

*"Buy land. They're not
making it anymore."*

– Mark Twain

S ome will say that 2008 changed everything. We say...yes and no. Although certain elements of real estate investment will likely never be the same—getting financing will certainly not be as easy as it was before the crash—the most important truisms remain: know your market and know yourself.

Both of us have loved real estate since a young age. Perhaps it sounds odd—how can kids love real estate? In our case, growing up in Ohio, we saw an ad in the 1980's for a Carlton Sheets seminar. The ad said you could buy real estate with little to no money down and then enjoy a passive income. Is it much more complicated than that? Of course. But we were curious, business-minded kids, so we went to the class. Now, more than 25 years later, our passion for real estate and belief in it as an investment tool remains. We own several properties together and we both view these investments as a crucial element of our retirement plans.

Unlike buying stocks or bonds, investing in real estate is *tangible*. There's risk, of course, but owning a lot, house, or condo is having something real that you can see and improve upon and, barring an act of God or once-in-a-lifetime recession, you won't see it lose its value overnight. History supports our country's preoccupation with buying and selling property for profit: according to the U.S. Census Bureau, real estate steadily rose in value from 1940 to the 2008 crash, rebounding in 2010.[26] Indeed, lessons learned from the Great Recession seem only to have whetted the appetites of investors hungry for a good deal: in 2012, investment property purchases made up 24 percent of all real estate sales, closing in on 2005's numbers.[27]

Six Questions to Ask Yourself Before Buying Real Estate

Thinking about buying a house to flip it, or perhaps renting out a few properties? Here are a few things to ask yourself first. Be completely honest when reflecting on these questions. Like any business, real estate is not necessarily a match for everyone's financial goals and personality.

1) Do you have a true passion for properties, and also a passion for bigger issues like how neighborhoods shift

26   Beattie, Andrew, "Simple Ways to Invest in Real Estate." Investopedia, 10/25/09.
27   HSH.com, "8 Costs to Consider When Buying a Rental Property." Nasdaq.com, 8/1/13.

over time and what makes a location attractive or not so attractive?

2) Are you someone who is interested in passive income? That's part of what interested us when we were younger and first saw the real estate seminar ad. We were working on our landscaping business, which did great but involved plenty of labor. Real estate, ideally, is a way to make money without physically doing the work. It's about your money doing the work for you.

3) Are you a patient person? Your money working for you doesn't mean you're doing no work at all. Having patience can be frustrating and nerve-wracking, but, as a real estate investor, it's part of the job requirement. If you're not comfortable with the idea of waiting, in some cases, years (or even a decade or two) for your real estate investment to really start upping your income, this field may not be a good fit.

4) Are you comfortable with putting a chunk of money somewhere and not touching it? While real estate is a great way to make your money work for you, to do it well and get the most out of the investment, it also means being comfortable with having money tied up— maybe for years or even decades.

5) Do you understand the pros and cons of leverage? Spend significant time reflecting on what this means in real estate. On one hand, using the bank's money to buy a property will earn you more money than you borrowed in the long run, ideally. The flip side is that the value of the house could go down (though the

severity of what happened in 2008 was historic), and if you can't sell it for more than you owe the bank, you end up with a big loss.

6) Are you willing to start with residential properties? Commercial properties can be excellent investments, but require significantly more experience and money because they come with many more risks. Risks in the commercial property market include: paying more money out of pocket, the fact that business properties statistically stay vacant longer, and the fact that many companies go out of business at a high rate (leading to potential fighting over rents/leases, less stability in income flow, etc.). Finally, the pool of people opening businesses is not remotely as large as the number of people who need a place to live.

Finally, let's run some simple figures to illustrate how to think about investing in a rental property:

- Purchase Price of a two-family dwelling in Happy-Ville USA: $100,000

- Immediate repairs: $15,000

- Closing costs: $5,000

- Total project costs $120,000

Let's assume the bank finances 75% of the purchase price ($90,000) and you put down the remaining $30,000. If you want to have at least a 10% return on your investment, you would need to net $3,000 a year after all expenses and debts are paid annually. Once you plug in the variables (mortgage rate, property taxes, insurance, etc.), you can determine if the market rent and operating expenses will support your investment.

Every situation will be unique—which is part of what makes the real estate game fun—but the key for us has been to always make our money on the buy. You never know what the future may hold, and even the most promising of markets may reverse course. Decide what your parameters are up front, do your research, and don't go through with a deal unless you can make money on it today.

Westlake Avenue: 20 Years of Ups and Downs

Todd and I embarked on our first rental property purchase over two decades ago, and we still own it today. This modest, two-story, two-family home in a rental-heavy suburb of Cleveland cost us $94,000 in 1995 As two kids scraping together our $5,000 down payment, we couldn't have known that this seminal property would, in time, leverage our entire real estate investment portfolio.

Although this sounds like a success story—and it is— owning the Westlake property has not been without its ups and downs. When our first tenant moved out after having lived there for years, Todd and I spent an extremely long, hot weekend scrubbing the curry residue off the walls with brillo pads. Our tenant must have cooked with the pungent spice for every meal. To this day, I cannot stomach the smell or taste of curry! This story illustrates not only the unexpected "surprises" a renter can leave you with, but is also an example of an instance when it probably would have made more sense to hire outside help. Maintaining a rental property often forces you to ask yourself which is more valuable: time or money? When I was single and unmarried—sure, I was happy to hop over and fix a light bulb. Later, when family needs demanded more of my time, it made sense to have a roster of dependable maintenance people on hand. To me, it's worth the extra outlay.

But the curry incident was nothing compared to the call I received at work one afternoon in 2006 from the Lakewood fire department. Apparently, the house was on fire. Not knowing what to expect, I raced over to stand with what seemed like half the town as I watched the firefighters douse the crumbling, charred first story. Happily, none of the tenants were injured. Unhappily, the fire—caused by someone leaving a cigarette burning—rendered both units uninhabitable. Although insurance paid a hefty sum, the house had to be gutted and rebuilt. The expenditures resulting from this calamity were both expected and unexpected: months of vacancy for both units was a foreseeable hit; the theft of the brand new, just installed copper plumbing is something I didn't expect. But having set aside all income made on the property into a reserve account, we were able to recover and get new tenants within a few months after the fire damage was repaired.

Still, there were more good times than bad. Despite the hiccups along the way, the income stream generated from the Westlake property has allowed us to invest in five more properties in Charlotte—an exciting market that Todd knows well. And over the course of 20-odd years of ownership, Westlake taught us a valuable lesson in real estate investing: be prepared for anything because stuff will happen. It's not the upsets and inconveniences that will sink you, it's being unprepared for them that will.

Todd: 8-Unit Apartment Building: Keeping Emotions at Bay

I love finding deals. In Charlotte, where I live, I am always on the hunt for a promising property. Not too long ago, I thought I'd uncovered a gem: an 8-unit apartment building whose current owners had bought at the peak of the market and were now suffering through 50% vacancy and banks threatening foreclosure. Surely, they would be thrilled to have this problem property taken off their hands.

The owners were indebted to two banks, which held a first and second mortgage of $250,000 and $50,000 respectively, a fact that really brought home the extent to which lenders were just giving away money before the crash! We ran the numbers and came up with a $125,000 value based on what we knew had to be done to the building. There was significant deferred maintenance, and each of the units was in need of a complete overhaul. Our estimate was $50,000 in repairs. This would put us at $175,000, and we knew each unit could be rented for $600/month (putting our gross annual income from the property at $57,600).

We presented our offer to the primary lender and the owner. To our surprise, they both agreed. The next step was the second mortgage holder. The owner approached this bank and offered to pay off $25,000 of the $50,000 balance. They initially declined but after Chris discussed it with them further, they knew this was the most they would ever get since any sale price in the future would have to pay off the first mortgage holder before them.

We were excited! With the signed contracts in hand, we explored our financing options and ordered the inspection with eyes wide open, knowing that each unit needed a lot of work. But, hey—we'd budgeted for that from the start. Or had we? The inspection killed us: it came back showing an additional $40,000 worth of repairs were needed on top of the $50,000 for which we'd already budgeted. My instinct was to move forward with the purchase regardless—we'd come so far and invested so much time and energy already! But Chris was reluctant to spend more on the building then we had originally agreed to. We ultimately decided to go back to the seller and ask for a reduction in the price to $100,000, but he declined saying he had a back-up offer. We walked away.

Even though I tell my clients not to get emotionally attached to real estate, in this case, I found myself in that exact position. Chris and I will never know if we passed up the deal of a lifetime, but we do know that as painful as it may seem in the moment, coming up with a plan and sticking to it is a matter of integrity for our partnership that will serve us well on future deals. It is very easy to get attached to a piece of real estate and compromise your original agreement to stick to a certain price and certain criteria. Often, it takes someone else to hold you accountable.

9 Ways to Win the Real Estate Game

Real estate does involve some luck and timing, but we've found that never deviating from these nine critical philosophies is what has helped us see success.

1) Start small, especially if you're more risk-adverse. A good option here would be a condo in an area where you have personal knowledge of the rental market.

2) Don't buy a property unless you can hop in the car and go see it. If you are far away, you are at the mercy of property managers and maintenance people, some of whom you may not know. Better to be able to assess the situation yourself and call upon a trusted source for help.

3) Maintain at least a 20-year outlook. That's the timeline we use for the properties we rent instead of flip. It will take about that much time for the rent to pay off the mortgage so until that point, you really won't be making much money on the property. (We avoid 30-year mortgages and are committed to paying down our properties faster than most people do.

Aggressive amortization may be something for you to consider as well.)

4) We always have a plan before entering into an investment, and for us—and for you—a plan must involve specific numbers. Don't say, "If it doesn't rent soon, we'll drop it a bit." Instead, run the numbers and be able to make a definite plan based on them, such as, "If the apartment doesn't rent in the next three months, we'll drop our asking price by $100/month."

5) Turn off HGTV. Remodeling shows and magazines can have some interesting ideas, but they spotlight the most extreme cases and often make exaggerated claims about potential returns—and often downplay the real costs of a project. We don't recommend putting a lot of money into trendy upgrades. Keep it simple.

6) We typically buy condos or homes in the $75,000-$125,000 range. Now, we're talking about markets in places like suburban Cleveland and Charlotte, NC, not North Dakota or New York City. Point being: You can get a decent little place for that amount of money in our markets. We don't typically buy below that amount because, for our markets, it signals a problem property or a bad neighborhood. Spending above that range and covering our monthly mortgage and expenses starts to require a rent amount that excludes too many potential tenants, making the property harder to keep filled. These numbers are all about thorough knowledge of the markets where you are buying, something you must research.

7) Don't get greedy, lazy, or too comfortable. Yes, it seems so obvious, but we're all human. The tricky side of getting good at something and gaining experience is that the better someone gets at any skill, it's easier for him to forget the basic principles or to start thinking the rules don't apply to him. A lot of people who got burned in the 2008 crash weren't rookie flippers, but people with 20 years of experience in real estate. They just hadn't gone into their investment with a back-up plan. Before you buy, you always need a back-up plan detailing how you can recoup as much money as possible for a property if needed, period.

8) We budget for both short-term and long-term maintenance. Short-term means fixing the lights before offering a property up for rent. Long-term means if we know we want to own a property for 20 years, it's inevitable at some point we'll need to pay to have the roof replaced, the HVAC systems replaced, etc.

9) Make choices that reflect your lifestyle and time. When we were younger, unmarried and childless, we bought properties where we did the fixing up ourselves, and also screened the tenants. That involved a huge amount of time and some headaches, but we wanted to be in real estate and we didn't have extra cash to hire help. We're in our 40s now, with young children, a busy family life, and full-time careers outside of the rental properties. Today, most of our properties are repaired and managed by people we hire. It's worth more to us to hire someone now to handle all those odd jobs because it frees up hours we can spend with our families, and, unlike in our 20s, we have enough

money to pay someone else to fix a deck or an attic. Time versus money is one of life's great debates, so if you're interested in real estate, ask yourself how much time you are willing to put into it and whether you can afford to outsource maintaining the property.

Investing With a Partner: Should You Do It?

As you've gathered from this book, we work together well on a personal and professional basis, and have a lot of mutual trust. That's made our joint real estate investments relatively easy. But as we discussed in the previous chapter, that's not often the case. Investing in real estate alone is just fine, of course, but if you're interested in partnering up with someone, here are three things you must discuss.

1) What's our ideal outcome here? Again, don't stop at broad statements like "to make money." Dig deeper to get the numbers, the data, and the big picture. Such as: "To rent this condo for $100 more than our monthly expenses (mortgages, taxes, repairs), to pay off the mortgage within 15 years, and then to keep the condo as a rental indefinitely after the mortgage is paid off."

2) What's our worst-case scenario here? We recommend creating a contract—in writing—that spells out when and why one partner might want to get out of the ownership.

3) Who gets the call? Even if ownership is joint, you must pick someone to be the "point person." That's the person the plumber, the tenant, the property manager, or the bank calls.

When a Hot Market Can Spell Trouble for You: Red Flags

A great market is, well, a great market! It's wonderful to sell high or have renters outbidding each other.

One thing to watch for? Markets with low inventory will fuel a flipping market. Loose credit standards will also generate larger amounts of flippers, as we saw in 2008. Like many things, flipping markets and generous lending are not necessarily bad—but they can lead to big problems. Once the inevitable stall or tumble happens—and it happens in almost every housing market every five to seven years—values will halt or drop, and foreclosure rates will increase. If you're interested in real estate, those elements are market factors you need to be prepared to have the stomach to ride out. History proves that property values always bounce back. Even if you are tempted to sell out of fear of a further slide in value during a crash or downturn, it can be wise to resist giving in to that emotion. As the saying goes: "Stay calm and carry on!"

We wish you the best of luck should you decide to dabble in or make a career out of real estate investment. We believe in it, work hard at it, and hope to ultimately retire happily off of it. With the right temperament, knowledge, and willingness to work, you can, too.

Pearls of Wisdom

- Make your money on the buy.

- Know your market, know your market, and... know your market.

- Be prepared for anything, because things will happen.

- Don't let your emotions lead you into poor decision-making.

- Be patient.

Chapter 10:
Learning to Accept Risk and Cultivate Resilience

"Do not wait to strike till the iron is hot; but make it hot by striking."

–William Butler Yeats

All business and investing decisions involve **risk.** Heck, all of life involves risk. So what are we supposed to do? After all, it's not safe to keep a ship at a dock all the time—the bottom will rust out.

Learning how to evaluate your own risk tolerance is an important skill. Even more important is learning how to ride out the ups and downs without losing your equilibrium—because every market will have an up and down at some point. These are tricky things to master, but they are the tickets to self-confidence in your financial choices and maximum success with your money.

Risk is sneaky: We're biologically hard-wired to focus on short-term risks, not long-term ones. This makes sense; in the animal world short-term risks are a matter of life or death. But in business and investing, we must strengthen our critical thinking skills in an area that isn't as instinctive. We have to think long-term. Remember, what looks like overnight success from an outsider's point of view probably took at least 15 years to accomplish. Why is that important to keep in mind? Because luck does happen, but in most cases, people make their own luck with a lot of hard work, perseverance, and patience. As the old Chinese proverb goes: "Pearls don't lie on the seashore. If you want one, you must dive for it."

Tips on Assessing Risk When Launching a Business or Other Investment

When you have a fresh idea or plan for making money, it's natural to be excited. In fact, the more passionate you are, the more likely you will be to dive right in. Having passion for your life and your work is fantastic. But this is where planning—even if it means slowing down—is key. Just like the rose-colored glasses we all wear when in the throes of a new romance, it's easy to ignore or underestimate potential red flags at the beginning of a project about which you feel enthusiastic. Whether you're looking to launch a small side business or something much bigger, a thorough assessment of the risks and pitfalls of any financial decision will help make your passion a success.

Here are a few risk-related tips to consider before launching a business.

1) Concepts such as scope, timeline, budget, tasks and milestones will help you to form a concrete, specific business plan. This is your essential map for predicting and minimizing risk. Commit to revisiting your business plan at least once a quarter in order to account for any changes that have occurred. This will keep your vision dynamic and flexible.

2) Once you've identified your risks (and if you haven't come up with at least four, you're not thinking hard enough), ask yourself how likely those risks are, and how well you can control the event if it does happen. If you can, assign specific dollar amounts those risks could involve.

3) Make sure you have tools to measure risk. The beginning of an investment, especially starting a small business, is usually the riskiest time. But a smart moneymaker will always be looking on the horizon for new challenges that may arise as a company grows or changes.

4) Learn how to handle your emotions. There's no right or wrong here, but choose the healthiest way to handle any stress or worries. For some people, that means turning off CNBC. For others, it's taking a walk or meditating.

5) Is your venture an instant success? Congratulations, but make sure you don't become over-confident when

you do well. You're not always going to win, and being able to learn from setbacks is the difference between a life-long career and a short one.

We often hear that great risk is the way to achieve great reward. While this can be true, sometimes it is not practical, and it misses out on something else: The cumulative impact of many small risks can build your confidence and savvy, making you more prepared to take bigger risks in the future, and more resilient if those larger risks don't work out. If you are not accustomed to taking risks in your financial life, it is important to start small. This can build confidence and prove that risk can be beneficial to your business.

Todd: Risky Business, an International Wine Venture

Studying abroad in Austria and Germany as an undergrad was a life-enhancing experience for me. It's an extraordinary way to learn about the world and also increase one's self-sufficiency, confidence, and appreciation for other cultures. So when Chris and I were getting our MBAs at Case Western Reserve University and I learned our program had an option for study abroad, I jumped at the chance for another great experience. Chris had never been abroad, and I wanted him to take advantage of this opportunity. Next thing we knew, plans for us to study in Hungary were developing.

An interesting thing happened before we left: We found a professor who would give us some flexibility by allowing us to create an independent study project while in Hungary. He also mentioned something else: Hungary's wine industry. Hungary had a long history of making quality wines, he said, but little was exported—a fact that had inspired him to launch a business exporting these wines. His attempt floundered, but we knew if we tried harder, worked it a different way, there was a chance of success. Keep in mind this was in the 1990s, when parts of Central and Eastern Europe were just emerging from decades of communist control. The region was a rapidly changing place.

Chris and I were by no means wine connoisseurs, but our professor's descriptions soon got us excited as we began our own research. Very few Americans were doing business in or travelling to Hungary at this point, and small, quality wineries there had a chance to export— but they weren't. There was a sense of Hungary's wine industry being in a grassroots kind of place, and that we could enter it at a pivotal time.

We hadn't planned to launch a business in Hungary while studying abroad, but it seemed like too good an opportunity to miss. We learned that Poland was a non-wine producing country, and because it was relatively close by, it seemed like a good place to start exporting Hungarian wine.

We put our hearts into a business plan for an exporting business: financial analysis, marketing, everything. And wouldn't you know it: The International Winefest was taking place the weekend we arrived in the country. To two eager 26-year-olds, it felt like serendipity. I spoke German, which some people there spoke, and a lot of people knew some English. We went around and pretty much said, "Hey, we're from Cleveland. We have this business plan, can we talk to you?"

Soon we were visiting these incredible boutique wineries across the country. We focused on a niche market that would involve higher quality wines in smaller quantities than the established mainstream wines in Hungary.

Our initial work wasn't without complications, of course. We faced questions such as: How do you set up an LLC in Hungary (a Limited Liability Company is a common way to set up a small business)? And going back and forth between Hungary and Poland was no small feat given the hurdles of foreign travel, language snafus, and ever-present pickpockets. But we still had so much excitement, and every step of putting it together felt fulfilling. Even though we'd already had the successful landscaping and investment property experiences together, Chris and I were happy to discover we were a great team on the wine enterprise too. We split costs 50-50 as we went along the way.

Once back in the U.S.—my time in Hungary extended to a year and a half — we needed money. I was living at home and didn't have a job. I knew if this business was going to work, we needed to be all in or all out. We decided to focus on bringing these niche wines to the

U.S. at that point rather than trying to get into Poland, which would have required more time abroad.

We had 15 cases, which we used as samples, brought in to Cleveland. We had to make the decision: Do we bring in more? How many more cases? 500 cases? At the time, Cleveland had the second-highest Hungarian population outside of Budapest. But what we were discovering was that the native Hungarians' tastes weren't as discerning as someone used to drinking California wines—they wanted their familiar brands, even if those brands weren't nearly as good. And even if the general, non-Hungarian public would have loved these wines, we had trouble getting into grocery stores, because those stores required a huge volume.

It was around this point that Chris decided to pull out. We were sitting around the dining room table, looking at how many bottles we'd need to sell in the U.S. to break even, and he didn't think it was going to happen. I didn't take it personally. Chris and I have a very open relationship, and we know how to keep our business and personal relationship distinct.

At this point I moved from Cleveland to Charlotte to get into the real estate business, and gave myself a year of working on the wine business solo. I did wine tastings at local wine shops and museum events. I decided I needed to go to California, New York, and Washington, D.C., to find distributors and shops there, and I did more tastings. I went to New Orleans for a big wine industry event; I got a booth, banner, spent a few thousand, everything. I just knew the wines were so good that once people tried them, the big break would happen. And I did get some decent leads, but ultimately, nothing panned out. I know now that I overextended myself. If I'd focused on one city it would have been much easier.

Soon another big business challenge became clear, beyond the volume issue: While I had correctly projected my costs for shipping from Europe to here, I'd miscalculated the costs of shipping wine within different cities in the U.S—and the cost of climate-controlled storage.

I didn't have the money to keep traveling, to say nothing of needing to work my other job. Part of me didn't want to let the business go because I knew it could work. Even now, 15 years later, I know it could work. I'd never not succeeded, never given up on something. But it just had become too expensive and I couldn't keep sinking my money into it. I just couldn't move the volume needed to sustain a business.

Chris and I still recall our adventure as a happy and memorable one. We learned a lot, but it was never meant to be our full-time, life-long business. If we had it to do over again, we'd probably partner up with someone who had deep pockets or tackle it when we had more resources of time and money ourselves. I wouldn't take that type of risk on an unproven business now. I learned important business questions that need extra attention and insight: What is revenue potential? When does revenue come in? What is the risk of this not working? What are the costs associated with starting this business? How much debt am I comfortable taking on? How long am I willing to stay in this business? What will have to happen for me to throw in the towel? Had I asked myself these questions—and been disciplined about answering them—perhaps I would have done things differently, or at least had different expectations.

I sold the rest of the wine wholesale to unload it, and left the experience with a big debt on my credit card. What's important here is that while I knew I needed a plan to pay down the debt efficiently, taking on debt as a business person didn't faze me. This isn't to say the debt wasn't stressful, but because I'd taken on business debts before and still made money, like in real estate purchases or even the equipment for our landscaping company, I didn't feel defeated or scared after the wine business. That's because I'd already had successes and I could draw on those experiences and the confidence I'd earned from them. Those prior successes helped me view the wine business as "win some, lose some, learn the lesson, do better next time."

Chris on Resilience: Cultivating Grit Through the Hard Times

Resilience is the ability to recover from or adjust to misfortune or change. Like our failed wine enterprise, some risks just don't pan out. It is how you handle such circumstances that really matters. Psychologists have identified some of the factors that make someone resilient. At the top of the list: optimism. Looking toward the future with hopefulness and gratitude can set the right tone for success. Change is an inevitable part of life and sometimes it sure can be painful. But by learning how to cope with misfortune you can turn a hardship into something valuable: a lesson to carry forward into your next venture.

Some people seem to be naturally blessed with resilience or, to use another word for it, grit. The good news: perhaps even more than talent, resilience can be cultivated and strengthened. If you want to be successful, you're going to need resilience, because everyone experiences setbacks both big and small.

The recent financial crisis hit many people hard, so I know I was not alone in enduring this difficult time. As the real estate market tanked, my investments that had looked so promising in 2007 floundered. In the throes of it, it was certainly challenging to see the Great Recession for the opportunity it was—a chance to develop and prove my resilience. You never really know how much endurance you have until you are faced with a crisis. I am fortunate that my upbringing was full of lessons on cultivating resilience, a quality valued by my parents. I had learned at a young age that being persistent through trying times was the key to successfully moving forward.

Do I wish the financial losses I experienced had never happened? It's not a question I ask myself. Dwelling on not achieving the outcome I once desired is unhelpful. Instead, I adapt and move forward, with my eye on a new desired outcome. But being persistent and optimistic— at least for me—doesn't happen in a vacuum. It has been critical for me that during the difficult periods of my life I have had a strong family and social network upon which to rely. These trusted individuals were my source for wisdom, perspective, and emotional support.

Though my children are still relatively young, I often imagine what I would say to one of them if he or she came to me as a young adult with a certain situation that was challenging his or her resilience. Here is how I would drill down the issue:

- What is going on? Find out the circumstances of his situation. Don't spoon feed the answer to him but drill down on what the true issue is.

- What are the facts (distinct from your emotions and feelings)? Get very clear on what is happening.

- What options do you have? What are the possible actions you could take? Brainstorm some actions. Should you stay the course, you could ask for help, give up...come up with options. What has people feeling trapped is when they don't have options.

- Do some thinking about each course of action and ask what they think will happen and then ask, What is your desired outcome?

- Which of those desired options is most likely to get you your desired outcome?

Cultivating resilience is a daily endeavor. Once you are able to express what your goals are, you can work toward them each day, adapting as the currents shift.

Consider doing a "check in" with yourself in order to stay on track. When you wake up in the morning, what do you tell yourself you are going to do? Are you happy with it? Do you go to work just to go to work and collect a paycheck and do the same thing the next day waiting for a weekend? Or are you fulfilled in your daily activities and striving for something more? Are you contributing to your overall goal, whatever that might be? These questions—and others you may think of on your own—can help you live an intentional life made richer by your grit and persistence.

Pearls of Wisdom

- Slow down. Don't dive into a new endeavor without assessing all the risks.

- Small risks can be just as valuable as larger gambles.

- Sometimes it's wise to cut your losses and get out if the venture isn't looking viable.

- Consider failure a form of helpful feedback. Even after a misfortune, resilient people are able to change course and soldier on.

Chapter 10: Learning to Accept Risk and Cultivate Resilience

Appendix A:
Illustration of Compound Interest

Age	Begin Balance	Salary (Increases by 3%/Yr.)	Save (12%/Yr.)	Earnings (8%/Yr.)	End Balance
22	$0	$50,000	$6,000	$480	$6,480
23	$6,480	$51,500	$6,180	$1,013	$13,673
24	$13,673	$53,045	$6,365	$1,603	$21,641
25	$21,641	$54,636	$6,556	$2,256	$30,453
26	$30,453	$56,275	$6,753	$2,977	$40,183
27	$40,183	$57,964	$6,956	$3,771	$50,910
28	$50,910	$59,703	$7,164	$4,646	$62,720
29	$62,720	$61,494	$7,379	$5,608	$75,707
30	$75,707	$63,339	$7,601	$6,665	$89,972
31	$89,972	$65,239	$7,829	$7,824	$105,625
32	$105,625	$67,196	$8,063	$9,095	$122,784
33	$122,784	$69,212	$8,305	$10,487	$141,576
34	$141,576	$71,288	$8,555	$12,010	$162,141
35	$162,141	$73,427	$8,811	$13,676	$184,629
36	$184,629	$75,629	$9,076	$15,496	$209,201
37	$209,201	$77,898	$9,348	$17,484	$236,032
38	$236,032	$80,235	$9,628	$19,653	$265,313
39	$265,313	$82,642	$9,917	$22,018	$297,249
40	$297,249	$85,122	$10,215	$24,597	$332,060
41	$332,060	$87,675	$10,521	$27,407	$369,988
42	$369,988	$90,306	$10,837	$30,466	$411,291

Age	Begin Balance	Salary (Increases by 3%/Yr.)	Save (12%/Yr.)	Earnings (8%/Yr.)	End Balance
43	$411,291	$93,015	$11,162	$33,796	$456,249
44	$456,249	$95,805	$11,497	$37,420	$505,165
45	$505,165	$98,679	$11,842	$41,361	$558,367
46	$558,367	$101,640	$12,197	$45,645	$616,209
47	$616,209	$104,689	$12,563	$50,302	$679,073
48	$679,073	$107,830	$12,940	$55,361	$747,374
49	$747,374	$111,064	$13,328	$60,856	$821,558
50	$821,558	$114,396	$13,728	$66,823	$902,108
51	$902,108	$117,828	$14,139	$73,300	$989,547
52	$989,547	$121,363	$14,564	$80,329	$1,084,440
53	$1,084,440	$125,004	$15,000	$87,955	$1,187,395
54	$1,187,395	$128,754	$15,450	$96,228	$1,299,073
55	$1,299,073	$132,617	$15,914	$105,199	$1,420,186
56	$1,420,186	$136,595	$16,391	$114,926	$1,551,504
57	$1,551,504	$140,693	$16,883	$125,471	$1,693,858
58	$1,693,858	$144,914	$17,390	$136,900	$1,848,148
59	$1,848,148	$149,261	$17,911	$149,285	$2,015,344
60	$2,015,344	$153,739	$18,449	$162,703	$2,196,496
61	$2,196,496	$158,351	$19,002	$177,240	$2,392,738
62	$2,392,738	$163,102	$19,572	$192,985	$2,605,295
63	$2,605,295	$167,995	$20,159	$210,036	$2,835,491
64	$2,835,491	$173,035	$20,764	$228,500	$3,084,755
65	$3,084,755	$178,226	$21,387	$248,491	$3,354,634

Chris and Todd age 5

www.ingramcontent.com/pod-product-compliance
Lightning Source LLC
Chambersburg PA
CBHW070931210326
41520CB00021B/6887